# Hands Off!
## This May Be Love

# Hands Off!
## This May Be Love

Gila Manolson

Lifecodex Publishing Company

Copyright © 2013 Gila Manolson.
All rights reserved.

Published by Lifecodex Publishing, LLC.,
Mercer Island, Washington.

No part of this publication may be reproduced, stored in a retrieval system, or transmitted in any form or by any means, electronic, mechanical, photocopying, recording, scanning, or otherwise, except as permitted under Section 107 or 108 of the 1976 United States Copyright Act, without the prior written permission of the Publisher.

Requests to the Publisher for permission should be addressed to Lifecodex Publishing LLC. PO Box 58, Mercer Island, WA 98040. Email: thoughttools@rabbidaniellapin.com.

Library of Congress Control Number: 2013938090

ISBN: 978-0-9822018-2-4

Printed in the United States of America

To my husband,
the love of my life

# CONTENTS

Foreword .................................................................. 1
Introduction ............................................................ 7
1. What's the Problem? ........................................ 13
2. God's Superglue ............................................... 19
3. Now You See It—Now You Don't ................. 28
4. Game Playing .................................................... 40
5. The Strongest Love Potion ............................. 51
6. Where's the Romance? ..................................... 58
7. Going for the Best ............................................ 66
8. The Experience Myth ...................................... 73
9. A Heart in One Piece ...................................... 85
10. It Means Nothing to Me ................................. 94
11. We're All in This Together ............................ 106
Conclusion: Moving Forward ............................ 121
Acknowledgments ............................................... 128
End Notes ............................................................ 129
Gila Manolson .................................................... 136

# FOREWORD

As I sat in the auditorium, I wasn't self-conscious about the tears rolling down my cheeks. No one was noticing them. They were too busy sniffling and wiping their own eyes. Along with 10,000 others, I had just watched a video showing a revered and beloved man explain that he was stepping down as president of the Bible college to which he had devoted his life. The reason? His wife was suffering from Alzheimer's disease and while she no longer recognized him, she was less agitated when he sat by her side holding her hand.

Why were we crying? Certainly, the love shining from the man's face and the adoration he was showing to a wife who was no longer able to reciprocate his devotion, touched us all. Nevertheless, I think another factor was at play. In an often cynical world, where announcements of divorce, abandonment and betrayal surround us, the video was a beacon of inspiration. It gave each of us in the audience the hope that we too could be part of a faithful, joyous and life-long love.

Truly, is there anyone who does not want to know that there is someone in the world who will stand at our side in the good times and bad, who will put a relationship with us ahead of all else and who will love us unconditionally? Yet while we may yearn for such an outcome, too few of us understand how to get on the path to achieving it.

The retiring man's touch on his wife's hand was enough to

bring her solace. Indeed, we know that the power of touch makes a difference not only in the elderly but also in a premature infant's survival. Unfortunately, as Gila Manolson reveals in this book, we frequently do not give touch the awe and respect it deserves during other phases of our lives as well.

There are many steps on the road to lasting love. One of the first is treating ourselves—and others—as worthy of such a blessing. Using both anecdotal and scientific examples, Gila shows that by cherishing our sense of touch and reserving the power, purpose and passion it encompasses for the right time and place, we can enhance our chances of being part of our own greatest love story ever told.

Susan Lapin<br>
Mercer Island, Washington

## Foreword

When a sperm touches an egg, the limitless potential of a human being is triggered. The chromosomes carried by the sperm and egg combine and soon the tiny zygote starts dividing repeatedly. Nine months later a bouncing baby will begin its journey into the world, a journey that began when a sperm touched an egg.

When toxic sodium and chlorine atoms touch, they combine into sodium chloride, otherwise known as common table salt, without which no plate of fries can be considered complete. The power of these two atoms touching produces an energy gradient that transforms two poisonous substances into a vital and tasty condiment.

Each time you start your car or turn on a light you are utilizing the amazing power of touch. That starter button or switch is nothing more than a mechanical device that makes one electrical conductor touch another. That touch allows an electrical current to flow from the battery to the starter motor or from the power source to the light bulb. The car surges to life or the dark room lights up due to the magic of touch that allowed energy to flow.

Nothing much would happen to a big, lonely ball of uranium. However, if another twenty-five pound ball of uranium touched it, critical mass would be instantaneously achieved and the fifty pounds of radioactive metal would begin a nuclear fission process that could produce enough energy to light a town. It could also unleash sufficient energy to destroy that same town.

Touch causes creativity, transformation, and energy. Touch

is an immensely powerful force in the universe. Like all powerful forces, it can produce positive change but it has just as much potential to devastate and destroy.

Touch is a waypoint on the road to intimacy, and as anyone who has loved knows, intimacy can release rapture and joy but it can also cause anguish and despair. Like all powerful forces, to make it safe and productive, intimacy must be harnessed and channeled. Unrestrained intimacy can burn itself out like a plunging meteorite. Intimacy without structure can result in embarrassment and awkwardness.

Not for nothing does royal etiquette in the United Kingdom prohibit any unsolicited touching of Her Majesty the Queen. Even a handshake has to be initiated by the monarch. Extending one's hand or taking her elbow to guide her, not to mention an unthinkable hug, would count as a colossal breach of etiquette. No anachronistic court custom, this recognition of the power of touch is a wise determination to keep it strictly under control.

Similar awareness is at play when a business professional tries to decide whether putting a friendly arm around an associate's shoulder would be appropriate. If appropriate, it could ease the way to agreement. If performed at a premature state of the relationship it could well destroy all potential.

So it is with early stage romantic relationships. Touch is a powerful force and pressing the wrong buttons at the wrong time can jeopardize all potential. No sane person would dabble with dangerous chemicals or fiddle with powerful machines having neither knowledge nor qualification. Similarly, sane people navigating the maze of romance need prior knowledge and qualification in understanding the power of touch.

Sadly, however, it is clear that across vast swaths of the culture, the genie of touch is out of its bottle and unrestrained. It whirls its way through society sowing sadness and causing pain. I know with utter certainty that the timeless truths of the Bible are needed now and in this arena.

Together with my wife, Susan, I am enormously proud to be the publisher of this indispensable guide to the power of touch. We knew of Gila Manolson and greatly admired her many achievements, hardly daring to think we might persuade her to write a book for our audience. At the moment she agreed, we knew we would have the privilege of bringing to the general public an unprecedented glimpse into ancient Jewish wisdom's teachings on touch.

Our prayer is that this book should bless every reader, transform every heart, and ultimately play its role in healing the culture. That along the way it will help smooth the path to true love, we have no doubt.

Rabbi Daniel Lapin
Mercer Island, Washington

# INTRODUCTION

## Why I Wrote This Book

I am a Jewish woman who grew up in a typically secular home in the northeastern United States. My parents sent me to Sunday school at the local Reform Temple, but that was about it for my Jewish education. Because Jewish identity is not chosen as an act of faith but inherited from mother to child, one can be nominally Jewish and neither know nor believe in anything particularly Jewish. That described my family. To me, Judaism was an ethnic and vague emotional identification that didn't demand any practical observance—some nice values, maybe, but nothing more.

Furthermore, in my circles, traditional beliefs were often discarded in deciding those values. I recall a "Jewish position paper" from my Temple on a controversial topic that stated, "The Talmud says such-and-such… Maimonides says such-and-such…Later rabbis say such-and-such… But in our generation we believe we can do what we want." In that case, it didn't really matter what religion I was.

In short, I was never taught that traditional Jewish wisdom might be helpful in living a successful modern life.

After graduating college and working for a year, I got the itch to travel and took off for Europe. I ended up in Israel, where I soon encountered a form of Judaism different from anything I had imagined existed. God and spirituality weren't yet part of my vocabulary, so my interest in this "new" type of Judaism—a Judaism that saw the Torah as its guiding light—was sparked solely by my suspicion that it might have something valuable to say about how to lead a meaningful life.

The fact is, I felt conflicted about some of the secular values I'd grown up with. On the one hand, as a latter-day product of the sexual revolution, part of me mourned having missed the heyday of the movement. Why couldn't I have been born earlier? I wanted to destroy old sexual taboos, be a flower child and celebrate "free love." Although that era was past and idealism had faded, I saw no reason to give up on the "advances" that revolution had brought; and not believing in God or religious values, nothing moral stood in my way. On the other hand, I couldn't brush off the deep, unarticulated sense that somehow, physicality should be meaningful. It was largely my dissatisfaction with the modern world's commonly accepted approach to this powerful part of life that moved me to explore the Torah's teachings.

In a way, this book began writing itself on my first Tishah B'Av, the day of mourning commemorating the destruction of the First and Second Temples in Jerusalem. It was around two o'clock in the morning, and I was sitting on the roof of

*Introduction*

a very old building in the Jewish Quarter of Jerusalem's Old City, overlooking the Western Wall. I had recently heard that anyone who mourns the destruction of Jerusalem would rejoice in its rebuilding. That sounded like a pretty good deal. I gazed at the Temple Mount, the place where God's presence was once tangible, trying to grasp the loss of the Temple and experience true grief, maybe even enough to shed some tears. Pondering the priestly services that were no more—and about which I understood little—didn't induce any great sorrow, and being a vegetarian, I wasn't sure how mournful I was over being unable to offer animal sacrifices. Instead, I tried focusing on the sorry decline we've experienced in human interaction.

Almost immediately, my mind moved to male-female relationships. I had grown up in a society that extolled love between a woman and a man yet was often incapable of it. "What the world needs now is love, sweet love / It's the only thing that there's just too little of," the radio sang to us—while the divorce rate doubled. Sentiments about love can fly high, it seemed to me, but without knowing how to realize them, they're not worth much.

> *This book was born out of the desire to share what I've learned with all individuals, Jewish and non-Jewish, who are seeking wisdom on relationships.*

Indeed, the more I dwelled on it, the more I was struck by the utter lack of clarity that pervaded society, the illusions with which so many people entered into relationships, and the pain that resulted when things inevitably didn't work out. In this highly sensitive and critical area of life, wisdom was strikingly absent. While I was grateful for having been spared so much of what others suffered, I thought about the many good, sincere and sensitive people I knew who were seeking something real, meaningful and lasting, and yet, as victims of the times were experiencing failure and unhappiness. Even those not hurting outright were suffering subtle and irreparable damage to their sensitivity and trust. It was all so needless. Suddenly, I was overwhelmed by this vast human loss and I cried.

A few years later, after I'd revamped my entire approach to relationships—and to Judaism and God—God sent a wonderful man into my life, and I've been happily married ever since. My gratitude for the love I was blessed with only exacerbated my pain for the growing number of those people, both Jewish and non-Jewish, who hadn't found anything close to it.

Pain is a great spur to action—and so, after marrying, I decided to help others discover what I had discovered. For the first five years of our marriage, my husband and I (and growing family) had the privilege of living in the Old City of Jerusalem, not far from that building upon whose rooftop I had once cried. Our tiny apartment was graced with old stone walls and arched windows. As Old City buildings are separated only by narrow walkways, we could hear our neighbors singing traditional songs from our living room or, from our bedroom, hear another neighbor giving Torah

## Introduction

classes. We loved it.

The best part of living in the Old City was our proximity to the Western Wall where we would go every Friday at sundown to welcome the Shabbat, the Jewish Sabbath. The area was always packed. Tourists pressed notes into the cracks of the Wall while local residents swayed back and forth deep in prayer, or sang and danced celebrating Jewish unity by drawing secular soldiers into their circles. In the middle of the plaza, surrounded by scores of young students, kibbutz volunteers and backpackers, a very special man made sure that anyone who wanted could experience Shabbat dinner with a religious family. Every week he would call to ask how many guests we could take, and every Friday night we returned home with a group of strangers eager to share our Shabbat. All were interested in learning about Judaism—and more than anything else, I discovered, about Judaism's approach to relationships. In their cautious questions and in the pauses in the conversation, you could almost hear them asking, sometime even pleading, "Do you have something better to offer us?"

This book was born out of the desire to share what I've learned with all individuals, Jewish and non-Jewish, who are seeking wisdom on relationships. My hope is that it will help others find their way to true, life-long love that will be a source of blessing in their lives.

CHAPTER 1

# WHAT'S THE PROBLEM?

## Are We Happy Yet?

I'm very much a "people person" and like nothing better than being invited to speak to groups. One particular time, I was speaking on the campus of a well-known university. My topic, of course, was relationships—and my purpose was to challenge the current hookup culture and suggest ways of relating I felt would yield more long-term happiness and fulfillment. As expected, there was no shortage of questions—except from one young woman who gazed at me intently, her face slightly hardened, not uttering a word.

After the talk, some of the participants congregated outside. A friend of mine overheard the following conversation between the girl who'd sat silently and another female student.

"You were awfully quiet. What did you think of what she had to say?"

Pause. "Truthfully? It makes a lot more sense than what I've been going through."

Long pause, then quietly, "It's been a rough couple of years, huh?"

Deep, painful sigh. "Yeah."

Despite the portrayal of high school and college campus life as one big good time, a lot of people—especially females—will confide they don't find it so fun. Many will confess that their lives are driven less by personal desire than by social pressure—the proof being how many college women have to get drunk to hook up.[1] Even when personal desire is the motivating factor, somehow the results aren't as wonderful as expected.

> *Despite the portrayal of high school and college campus life as one big good time, a lot of people —especially females— will confide they don't find it so fun.*

Only a few generations ago, young women divided relatively neatly into "nice girls" and "naughty girls." While society gave boys more latitude, they too understood that there was a right and a wrong way to interact with the opposite sex before marriage. That's why mothers correctly told their daughters that a boy might happily play around with one type of girl but would marry only another. "Nice" girls didn't make out for the first few dates, didn't do more than that until they were "going steady," and didn't do more than *that* until they'd tied the knot. I'm talking mid-twentieth century here; in earlier times, even routine 1950's behavior would raise eyebrows.

Today, those once-accepted norms seem as outdated as whalebone corsets. The TV show *I Love Lucy* of the '50s, where Lucy and Ricky Ricardo's bedroom featured separate beds, gave way to *One Day at a Time* of the '70s and '80s, where divorced mom Ann Romano made the controversial decision to spend a weekend with a man, which eventually gave way to *Sex and the City* (which I probably don't have to tell you about). We can't begin to fathom how this has impacted our sensitivities. Viewing sex as mere recreation has become so normative that no matter how sheltered we may be, we can't help but be affected. Among others, we can thank for this Helen Gurley Brown, long-time editor of *Cosmopolitan* magazine, who until her death at age ninety promoted promiscuity as the optimal lifestyle for both men and women. Today it doesn't need to be promoted; it's a given.

Even those who should be the most innocent have fallen victim to new sexual mores. On conservative and religious college campuses with strict student codes, the news of couples sleeping together isn't greeted with the universal shock it would have aroused in previous years. Girls who wear purity rings and boys who have pledged to save sex for marriage still see movies and read books that present cohabitation as expected and virgins as dinosaurs.

At the secular end of the spectrum, casual sex and hooking up has replaced relationships. Already in middle school, boys and girls randomly engage in sexual practices that I doubt my grandparents ever heard of. By high school, kids are losing their virginity en masse. On college campuses, what some students did a generation ago in the name of "free love," nearly all students are doing today, far more casually (and often drunk), in the name of no ideology whatsoever.

The result is that while we still crave intimacy—humans always will—fewer and fewer people have any clue how to achieve it, or even what it is. It's no surprise that when men and women do attempt real relationships, they often find themselves alone again too quickly, in pain and wondering what went wrong. We are all victims of today's sexual culture, and it is causing tremendous suffering.

## A Jerusalem Wedding

The purpose of this book, like the countless talks I've given, is to share the Torah's alternative for relationships. For there is a solution to the unhappiness I've witnessed. It's radical, but it just may be the most incredible tool there is for achieving a genuine connection with another. Furthermore, it's for anyone who wants it. "A light unto the nations," the prophet Isaiah called the Jewish people[2]—for God's message to His people was never meant to remain solely with the Jews. Wisdom on relationships is out there for the taking, for anyone who desires to make it his or her own.

In Judaism, this wisdom is called *shmirat negiah* (sh'mee-RAHT neh-gee-AH)—literally, "guarding touch."

I prefer a different translation. The Hebrew word *shmirah* can also mean "reserving" or "saving." Most beautifully, it can imply "cherishing"—for something we guard and reserve, something we save for a special time with a special person, is something we cherish.

Cherishing touch means that we save it—ideally, even the slightest bit of touch—only for our marital relationship.

I'll never forget my first encounter with this idea. I was a newly arrived tourist in Jerusalem when someone I met invited me to attend a religious Jewish wedding. (In Jerusalem, anyone and everyone can show up to "gladden the groom and bride" by participating in the incredibly joyful dancing.) I exchanged my jeans for a jean skirt and went. As I entered the hall, I saw the bride. She looked radiantly beautiful as all brides do. But something was very different about her, and I was struck by it. I had never seen a young woman look so pure and innocent. When I commented on this to the person who brought me, she informed me that perhaps it was because the bride *was* pure and innocent. Not only had she and her husband-to-be not had sex; they had never even *touched*. Neither had she touched any other man she'd dated.

> *While we still crave intimacy—humans always will—fewer and fewer people have any clue how to achieve it, or even what it is.*

Needless to say, I spend the rest of the wedding with my jaw agape. *Are you crazy?* I thought. *Are you brainwashed? How could you do that?*

Upon reflection, I realized that the "normal" approach to relationships wasn't producing spectacular results. Could this absurd-sounding practice actually make sense? I made up my mind to find out.

Little did I know that a few short years later, I would choose to date my husband-to-be in the same way.

I've found "cherishing touch" to be an amazing practice. Perhaps, in our sex-saturated society, it is the most powerful antidote to superficial or just plain wrong relationships there is. I've also been successful in getting large numbers of my fellow Jews to adopt it. This book, however, is addressed to Christians, Buddhists, agnostics and anyone else who is interested. God created every person on this earth with emotional and spiritual needs that don't dissipate in the face of new social mores. "It is not good for man to be alone," the Torah tells us,[3] and that is as true for all of us today as it was for Adam.

God loves us, and therefore He gave us the gift of touch along with directions on how to use it. This book describes, in a down-to-earth, common-sense way, how cherishing touch can help you achieve the real, lasting relationship I believe we all deeply want and that God wants for us.

CHAPTER 2

# GOD'S SUPERGLUE

## Subtle Sensations

Imagine yourself in the following situation. You and a stranger are having a heated argument. Tempers are rising, and soon you are practically shouting at each other. Realizing things are getting out of hand, your opponent interjects, "Hold on—let's try and calm down." It doesn't work. You are still furious. He or she leans forward, puts a hand on your arm, and says, "Wait a minute." Suddenly, for some reason, you feel powerless to continue screaming. Your anger abates and you concede, perhaps even resentfully, to the suggestion.

Now imagine yourself at a checkout counter. You always dread entering this store because it takes so long to get out. Today is no exception. You have been waiting for what seems like an eternity to pay for your purchase. Finally, your turn comes and you hand the slow-moving cashier your money. Usually you have to pick up your change off the counter, but today the cashier places it in your hand, and for a brief moment you feel the warmth of his or her hand on yours. Outside afterwards, you're aware of something strange. For some reason, you're feeling more warmly towards this store than before.

One more scene: You have just finished dining at a restaurant. The service has been exceedingly slow. Your waiter, Dave, finally brings the bill.

"Hope you enjoyed your meal," he says with a smile and a parting pat on the shoulder.

Watching him return to the kitchen, you feel a surge of generosity and leave a bigger tip than you had intended. On your way out, you comment to the manager about how little waiters earn for working so hard.

"It all depends," he replies. "Take this new guy, Dave. We don't know how he does it, but he pulls in at least thirty percent more in tips than anyone else."

In each of the above true incidents, researchers will say you have fallen prey to one of the most subtle yet powerful forces in human relationships: touch.[1]

Notice, incidentally, that not once was the contact sexual or even affectionate. Still, touch had an undeniable effect. It awakened within you warmth and receptivity, conscious or unconscious, toward the other person. It brought down the walls, leaving you feeling distinctly closer and more connected. It created a subtle, subliminal bond.

## Two into One

Touch could be called God's Superglue for Human Relations. Take two clean surfaces, and Super Glue® will immediately stick them together. God created touch between people to work the same way. Take two people unopposed to feeling closer to one another and touch between them will do the trick. Mysteriously, in an instant, they'll feel closer.

If even a simple touch can make this kind of impact, imagine something really good and sexual coupled with a healthy dose of physical and personal attraction. A little ripple of warm feelings can become an emotional tidal wave.

Why is a mere physical experience between a man and woman, pleasurable as it may be, often interpreted as something more in many people's minds (particularly women's, as we'll soon see)? Why does physical contact often translate into emotional connection?

Jewish mystical tradition teaches that Adam and Eve, the first man and woman, were created as one connected being and only later separated.[2] Deep down, in the recesses of our minds, we "remember" once having been one with another. Now that we're separate and alone, we yearn to regain that original oneness. As Kabbalah (Jewish mysticism) teaches:

> *Too many people have realized, too late, that passing up togetherness doesn't work as a lifelong choice.*

"Male and female are intended to illuminate together.... Only when they are attached to one another are they called a 'light.'"[3] God's message to us is simple: Togetherness is our natural state of being. That is when our energies are greatest.

As singles, therefore, no matter how many friends we have or parties we go to, we increasingly experience the ache of incompleteness—the feeling that, alone, we're just not "shining." Consequently, one of our strongest desires is to experience the wholeness, the sense of "coming home," of "illumination," that comes from reuniting with our missing half. Yes, we've been told that singlehood is just as viable an option as couplehood. In reality, there are even times in our lives when it may be preferable. Nevertheless, too many people have realized, too late, that passing up togetherness doesn't work as a lifelong choice. As much as some of us may try to deny it, humans have an irrepressible need to seek closeness with one, special, other person.

> *Because you want to <u>be</u> close, and physical contact makes you <u>feel</u> close, you are liable to believe that you <u>are</u> close.*

But here's the catch. Because you want to *be* close, and physical contact makes you *feel* close, you are liable to believe that you *are* close—while, in fact, feeling close and being close are quite different. Touch can skew your perception of reality to the point where you mistake skin-to-skin contact for a heart-to-heart connection, leaving you with delusions of intimacy where no true intimacy exists. When we want something badly enough we can fool ourselves into believing we have it, although what we have is only superficially similar to what we truly want.

## The Trust Hormone

That's the spiritual explanation for the power of touch. There's a chemical one as well.

Our bodies produce many neurohormones, chemicals that operate through the nervous system and affect our brains. One that gets a lot of press is oxytocin. Oxytocin has been touted as the "love hormone," but I'd call it the "feeling bonded" hormone. It's released by physical closeness and it makes us feel bonded to the person with whom we're experiencing this closeness. For example, when a woman gives birth her body is flooded with oxytocin, making her bond with her newborn.[4] When she nurses, waves of oxytocin strengthen this connection, leaving her utterly in love with her baby.[5] You can see the Divine wisdom here. If children are to survive, women have to care for them, and they're more likely to do that if they bond with them.

God also wants husbands and wives to stay together in the holy union called marriage. When a man and woman are physically intimate, He makes sure oxytocin is right there, performing its magic, making them feel at one and committed.[6] But intimacy isn't necessary to start the chemical flow; oxytocin is released by any form of physical closeness. Hugging will do it. So will holding hands. In fact, oxytocin is secreted even when two people just *touch*.[7]

Oxytocin would be powerful enough if it only created a sense of bonding. But it does more: It turns off skepticism, caution, and aversion. And it turns on sociability, generosity, and most significantly, *trust*—giving it its other nickname, the "trust hormone." After inhaling oxytocin from a nasal spray, people will even invest more money with strangers[8] and donate larger amounts to unknown phone solicitors.[9] In other words, under the influence of oxytocin, you can kiss your judgment goodbye.[10] This makes touch a serious proposition. Hence leading neuropsychiatrist Louann Brizendine's advice to women: "Don't let a guy hug you unless you plan to trust him."[11]

Why is her warning specifically to women? That has to do with biological sex differences. Estrogen, the female sex hormone, increases oxytocin's effect; testosterone, the male sex hormone (also responsible for sexual desire), diminishes it.[12] This "oxytocin disparity" is especially pronounced in early adolescence, when estrogen and testosterone levels soar. Consequently, young teenage girls are dangerously vulnerable to the power of touch, and they'll bond, trust and shelve judgment at the drop of a hat. Author Susan Kuchinskas spells it out: "Girls should learn that bonding is a likely effect of physical intimacy—not necessarily a response to the other person. The feeling is, 'He's the only one for me.' But the reality is, 'Because we touched, I now *feel* as if he's the only one for me.'"[13]

Most young teenage boys, on the other hand, while greatly interested in females, have little ability to bond with them.[14] Their hormones are leading them more toward conquest than toward connection. What to a girl may feel like love may to a boy be nothing more than another notch on his belt. In other words, boys and girls have seriously different goals when it comes to relationships.[15]

As males and females mature and their hormones settle down, the gap between their chemical realities narrows somewhat and their needs move closer. Most significantly, men become increasingly interested in and capable of a genuine connection with a woman, especially after marriage. When a man grows close to a woman, he feels protective of her, which triggers his attachment instinct.[16] But married men also have somewhat less testosterone than bachelors, allowing for a greater oxytocin response and therefore more intense bonding. (It remains unclear whether this is because marriage lowers testosterone levels, or because men with lower testosterone levels are more likely to marry.)[17]

Nevertheless, oxytocin affects females more than males. Women ignore this reality at their peril.

## Affection or Manipulation?

Since, in addition to bonding, oxytocin shuts down judgment and creates feelings of trust, physical involvement before marriage can be dangerous. It can leave you feeling connected to someone who is totally wrong for you. The danger is worse if Mr. Totally Wrong has no scruples.

My friend, author Wendy Shalit, was in a store when she spotted a book called *How to Succeed with Women*.

"I knew I had to have it," Wendy told me. "It was the Handbook of the Enemy, and I wanted to be up on his tactics!"

In it, she reports, the (male) authors essentially counsel their readers to exploit the female oxytocin response to their advantage. On a date, they explain, the woman's sizing up the man, looking for reasons why he's not good enough for her. He therefore has to get physical with her *fast*—because then, instead of looking for reasons why he's *not* the right one, she'll be looking for reasons why he *is*.[18]

For a female, in other words, touch is subliminally manipulative. The problem, of course, is that a woman manipulated in this way can end up not just badly hurt but badly used. With enough such experiences, she can lose her personal boundaries and sense of self.[19] One thing's for sure: She won't be happy. Most of those who suffer depression due to romantic involvement are women.[20] When it comes to relationships, women are simply more likely to get hurt. (As are higher-oxytocin males, as a loving young man whose girlfriend recently dumped him painfully reminded me.)

We humans are vulnerable. If touch is God's Superglue for human relations, it pays to remember that Super Glue® can join two pieces of a broken plate—or two of your fingers. Similarly, touch—and particularly the "more than casual" kind—can make you feel closer to someone, irrespective of who he or she is and whether a genuine bond is ever likely to develop between you.

That's undoubtedly one reason why, in the world's major religions, physical intimacy is reserved for marriage, where it is not only permissible and beneficial, but also sanctified. In Jewish thought, *no human activity is holier than marital sex*. As Herman Wouk so aptly wrote in his popular book *This Is My God*:

> "What in other cultures has been a deed of shame…or of physical necessity, or of high romance, has been in Judaism one of the main things God wants men [and women] to do. If it also turns out to be the keenest pleasure in life, that is no surprise to a people eternally sure God is good."[21]

Sexuality is one of God's greatest gifts to us. Anything this powerful and potentially beautiful must be handled carefully. With the right person at the right time, physicality can intensify love—and sanctity. With the wrong person at the wrong time (and even with the right person at the wrong time), it can wreak emotional and spiritual havoc.

CHAPTER 3

# NOW YOU SEE IT—NOW YOU DON'T

## The Gift of Safeguarding Objectivity

God designed humans in such a way that touch creates a bond. If you're smart, before bonding with someone, you'll make sure that bond reflects something genuine and is therefore one you really want. To gain that clarity, you really have to know who that other person is. That requires objectivity. Unfortunately, objectivity comes about as naturally to most humans as waltzing does to a hippo.

Imagine yourself at a party, chatting with two members of the opposite sex. One you find extremely attractive, the other not. You say something—and they respond identically. Whose response sounds better?

If the mere sight of a good-looking person sends your objectivity out for a coffee break, once you start touching, it steps out for lunch. From that moment on, you see what you want to see. You also don't see what you don't want to see. With unusual self-knowledge, a young woman I know said, "Once I was physically involved with a guy, my emotional connection to him had me jumping through hoops to tell myself everything was great."

While women are most likely to be misled by their emotions, men are more likely to be misled by lust. As a young man I know put it, "When I'd get physical with a woman, I'd lose all clarity. I'd try to make everything work around the fact of how great it felt."

Psychologists call this the "pink lens effect"—and it's unbelievably widespread. In fact, researchers say it's universal. I routinely ask college students the following: "How many of you have ever been in, or witnessed, a relationship where anyone observing from the sidelines would say, 'What in the world does she see in him?' or 'What in the world is he doing with her?'" Every time, every single hand goes up.

> *Imagine yourself at a party, chatting with two members of the opposite sex. One you find extremely attractive, the other not. You say something—and they respond identically. Whose response sounds better?*

An incident from some years ago has stuck with me because of what it reveals about the delusions physical closeness can create. After college, I considered applying to graduate school in clinical psychology. My uncle, a psychotherapist, invited me to gain a firsthand glimpse of the profession by participating in a group therapy session he was leading. Much of that evening focused on a woman of about twenty-five as she poured out her painfully conflicted feelings about her boyfriend.

"Sometimes he treats me great, and sometimes he treats me like dirt," she explained through her tears. "I know I love him, but half the time I'm so angry at him. One day I think we have such a wonderful thing going, and the next day I want to break up and never see him again."

Clearly, this guy was not so loveable and the relationship not so wonderful, but no one had the courage to tell her. Finally, my uncle spoke up.

"This guy is poison for you," he told her straight out. "Can't you see that?"

Taken aback by his forcefulness, she immediately reacted: "But sometimes it feels so good, so right being with him."

"Listen to everything you've said," my uncle persisted. "This is not what I would call a good guy or a healthy relationship."

She looked at him uncomprehendingly. "But I feel so close and connected to him."

In short, she couldn't hear the truth. She sensed something was wrong, but she couldn't see how wrong.

## Love is Blind—but Not Forever

People become enmeshed in unhealthy relationships for countless reasons. One huge complicating factor is the early introduction of physical involvement. As soon as such closeness occurs, that all-too-familiar rose-colored cloud descends, enveloping everything in the warm glow of feeling close. Once this bonding takes place, you can kiss much of your perspective goodbye. By the time this woman had detected serious flaws in her boyfriend, their physical connection had left her so emotionally attached to him that she could no longer step back and see reality in its entirety.

Physicality can blind you. But not forever. For the rose-colored cloud eventually lifts and illusions dissipate. Suddenly, you'll be looking into the eyes of Mr. or Ms. Wonderful and seeing him or her *very* clearly.

I once visited a relative who had recently married a man she'd been with for two years. She looked depressed.

"I don't think my marriage is going to last," she told me sadly.

"Oh no!" I exclaimed. "But you've been married only three months! What could you have possibly discovered that you didn't know the whole time you two were living together?"

She sighed deeply. "I just don't think he's intellectual enough for me."

I was speechless. When I was dating for marriage, I could usually size up a guy's brains within the first half hour or less. Why hadn't she seen the truth a long time ago? Then it hit me: She had been physically involved with her boyfriend from very early on in their relationship. While that rose-colored cloud was down, he probably sounded like a rocket scientist. After it lifted, she heard a resounding "Duh..."

"But I'm not ready to think about marriage anyway," you may counter. Who said you have to be? Even as a single, do you want to risk spending weeks, months, or years with the wrong person? Do you want a misguided relationship to influence your choice of residence, college, lifestyle, or even life goals? People will move thousands of miles away from family and friends, not attend the best university they could, or give up their peaceful country life for the noise of the city or their action-packed city life for the boredom of the country, just to be with Mr. or Ms. Wrong. When the blinders come off, they realize they've compromised their dreams on behalf of a relationship that could never last.

Being in touch with reality is crucial when you're getting to know someone you might end up spending a serious portion of your life with, whether or not you ever marry him or her. Your feet have to be firmly planted on the ground, not three feet above it, and your head must be in this world. Fostering illusions is foolish and dangerous. If accessing this realism precludes physical involvement, that's certainly better than involving yourself with the wrong person based on a romantic fantasy.

There's one sure-fire way to give yourself a huge advantage in preserving clarity and objectivity: Saving touch for marriage—cherishing it.

*If you don't touch before you're married, how do you know the two of you will be physically compatible? Shouldn't you try things out first?*

"Things" is a vague term, but the truth is, it doesn't matter. In a very innocent culture, people pondering marriage might have wondered, "How could you marry someone you haven't kissed?" In the '50s, when the intimacy permitted for a college-age "good girl" was "everything but" (with a serious boyfriend), the question undoubtedly was, "How could you marry someone you haven't done any heaving petting (i.e. fooling around) with?" Today, the norm is to do everything with anybody, not to mention anyone you're actually considering marrying. Accordingly, the question now incredulously asked by many is, "How could you possibly marry someone you haven't slept with?"

What I'm trying to point out is that there's nothing objective about the "need" to experience whatever it is with one's future spouse. It's simply a matter of popular mores. Back in the '50s, the average unmarried girl felt no great anxiety about saving sex for marriage, and the average boy wasn't uptight about committing to her. Even without intimate knowledge of each other men and women evidently felt secure in their choice of marriage partners. People were probably no less secure when they abided by a societal norm of even less premarital experience or none at all. Why must so many people today "try things out" before committing themselves?

"Ah," the skeptic may interrupt. "Did those old-time innocents have decent sex lives once they were married? Given the stigma of divorce back then, probably a lot of frustrated people resigned themselves to being stuck for life with someone who, they discovered too late, had all the sensual sophistication of a dead fish."

In other words, past generations, poor things, weren't given the socially sanctioned opportunity to collect essential data about a potential spouse and undoubtedly suffered the consequences. We, living in these fortunate and enlightened times, have access to such information. Shouldn't we profit from it?

Yet the popular need to "try things out" derives from much more than an unwillingness to forfeit a golden opportunity. The fact is, nearly all of us are victims, to one degree or another, of modern society's unnatural, unhealthy attitude towards sexuality.

To many people, this last statement will sound oddly reversed.

"Wait a minute," they'll object. "We're the ones with the healthy view of sexuality. We feel free to express ourselves with anyone we want. You religious people are the ones who treat sexuality as unnatural with all your dos and don'ts. How can you say we're victims?"

I say that because the secular approach to sexuality reflects a grave misunderstanding of human nature. As a result, it is failing dismally in producing large numbers of deeply happy and fulfilled human beings.

Modern society's fatal error lies in relating to the body independently of the spirit that animates it. This unfortunate phenomenon is particularly observable in the field of medicine, where doctors often treat the body with little or no regard for the soul, not realizing how much one's mental and spiritual state affects physical health.

People must be viewed in their wholeness. God created our bodies and souls to work together as one, with the soul defining one's identity and the body expressing it. Our dress, speech, and behavior should all reflect who we really are, deep within our innermost being. Only then can we be fully ourselves.

With this holistic perspective, we can draw a basic conclusion about sexuality: Physical intimacy devoid of emotional intimacy, whether that is holding hands, hugging, kissing or more, is not a true expression of self. Yet many naïvely assume that we *can* divorce body from soul. We're supposedly able to shove our cumbersome emotions (e.g., "I don't really feel so much for him/her") into the closet and sail onto the streets as liberated bodies, without feeling we've left our real selves—and our Godliness—at home. In many circles, this body/soul division has become so accepted that one can ask equally casually, "How good a tennis player are you?" and, "How good a lover are you?" without sensing the essential incongruity of the two questions. Sexuality has come to be viewed as something purely physical, unrelated to the spirit—an activity that, like sports, can be coldly rated in terms of performance.

> *Women are most likely to be misled by their emotions; men are more likely to be misled by lust.*

[handwritten annotation: SO TRUE]

We can now understand why people are so afraid to become involved with someone whose ability to "perform" looms as a big question mark. After all, would you commit yourself to a game of doubles tennis with a partner whom you'd never seen hold a racket?

The crucial mistake, of course, lies in this extremely unrealistic (not to mention crass) comparison. The physical side of a relationship is neither a sport nor a performance subject to a point-basis evaluation by some critic observing from the sidelines. It is a primary means of self-expression and cannot be viewed in isolation from the person as a whole.

In short, to those who defend the popular outlook on sexuality, I would reply that turning people into virtual split personalities is neither natural nor healthy. Just as more and more people are embracing a holistic approach to healing, we need a holistic approach to sexuality.

## A Compatibility Gamble?

At this point in a talk, what I'm saying usually rings true for many in my audience. I then take a tack that lets people answer the original question, "Shouldn't you try things out first?" for themselves.

"What do you think," I ask, "makes for a good physical relationship?"

People immediately volunteer answers:

"Trust."

"Caring."

"Communication."

"Feeling really connected and close."

"Wanting to make the other person happy."

"Most of you seem to feel," I suggest, "that the main ingredient is an emotional one."

There are nods.

"Anything else?"

Invariably, someone adds with a grin, "Technique."

Grins of agreement spread across many other faces as well.

"Okay. Now I'm going to describe two scenarios. In scenario number one, you decide to marry someone with whom you've been intimately involved throughout your relationship. Physically, you know exactly what you'll be getting. On the other hand, you've sacrificed considerable objectivity about your partner, and deeper aspects of your relationship have never developed half as much as they might have.

"Now you're married, and you have the satisfying physical connection you expected. But you're starting to see certain things about your partner that you haven't noticed before, or have overlooked. Eventually you realize that deeply ingrained aspects of his or her personality really bother or even upset you, and that he or she lacks qualities that you can't imagine spending the rest of your life without. This realization, in turn, begins to diminish your satisfaction with your intimate life, since beneath the physical pleasure you don't feel as close and connected as you once did. That's scenario number one."

I pause. There is usually silence as the looks on many people's faces tell me that (even without having been married) they know this scenario.

"Now for scenario number two," I continue. "You decide to marry someone with whom you've had no physical contact. Largely because of this approach, you've been able to maintain a great deal of perspective on who he or she is, and the relationship has had a lot of space to develop deeply on the intellectual, emotional, and spiritual levels. On the other hand, you don't know what to expect physically from your partner.

"Now you're married, and as you had anticipated, your spiritual relationship is great and getting better all the time. Unfortunately, your intimate life is not earning a place in the Fireworks Hall of Fame.

"Now, tell me—which situation would you rather be in?"

It doesn't take people much time to choose. Technique can be learned; who a person is can't. You can easily teach someone how to touch you in a way that feels good, much like you can tell a friend where and how hard to scratch your back when it itches. It's virtually impossible to teach someone how to be the kind of person you need him or her to be to satisfy your *non*-physical needs.

The emotional connection between you and another person will probably account for at least ninety percent of the pleasure and satisfaction you will experience in your physical relationship. This connection is based upon your each being the kind of person the other can love. Being loveable usually means having certain universally loveable traits, such as kindness, willingness to give, sensitivity, etc., and whatever specific traits each individual needs to feel that "special attraction." You don't have to get physical to determine whether this "ninety percent" exists.

The remaining ten percent could be called the "how-to's." These can easily be picked up after marriage by anyone with a healthy attitude towards sexual expression, a desire to please one's partner, a minimum of intelligence and a willingness to learn and communicate.

Prior physical knowledge is irrelevant to the success of a relationship, and may even interfere with it. Personal knowledge is what counts. For true physical intimacy is nothing more—or less—than an embodiment of emotional intimacy. Therefore, if your questions about your future spouse's real essence have been answered, you can relax, because the vast majority of your questions about your future intimate life have been answered as well.

CHAPTER 4

# GAME PLAYING

## You Make This Move; I Make That Move

Games are great if you're looking for fun, but not when it comes to relationships. As a matter of fact, they're downright non-productive. Unfortunately, they can be hard to escape.

When two people know that getting physical is part of the script for their relationship, a large placard appears in the wings, bearing, for all to read, the Schedule of Expected Increasing Physical Closeness. (Actually, I prefer to call it the G.A.M.E.—Generally Assumed Mating Expectations.)

You're probably grinning, knowing what I mean. In case you don't, let me explain. In every typical male-female relationship, it's understood that the physical side is going to progress according to a certain Schedule, given the norms within your particular social circle. If you're exceptionally wholesome, the Schedule may proceed very slowly and never pass a certain point before marriage. At the other extreme, sometimes a serious amount of activity is compressed into one casual get-together (witness the college campus hook-up scene). Whoever you are, there's a Schedule. Thus, as the evening wears on, you're increasingly thinking, "Okay, this is Get-Together Number X, which means that, sooner or later, we should be doing Physical Activity Y." This assumption prompts a whole flurry of mental activity ("what if she doesn't...", "what if he does...", "will my friends think I'm a loser if I don't...", "will my friends think I'm easy if I do...", "will she suspect I'm gay if I don't...", "should I at least give him something since he treated me to pizza..."), culminating in the big question (which is a question usually only for the female): "Do I want to?"

Here's where the major league games begin. If you're the boy (who usually plays quarterback), the challenge is how and when to make the appropriate move. If you're the girl (who usually plays receiver), things are trickier. For in this climate of expectations, whatever you do is likely to be read—or misread—as a red or green light.

For example, a young woman who preferred a slower Schedule than many of her peers told me, "When I first went out with a guy, I would just be my normal, super-warm self—and suddenly I'd notice a glint in his eye. I realized I had to curb my natural friendliness if I didn't want it to be 'misinterpreted.' But how do I do that without making him think I'm not interested?"

When touch is part of the picture, everything "means" something physical—and that may prevent you from being yourself because of what it may "mean."

Another frustrated woman describes it like this: "If I say 'Let's take a walk in the woods' (because I'm in a nature mood), he assumes I want to get away from other people so we can get physical and am therefore into him. If I say 'Let's go downtown' (because I'm in a city mood) he assumes I want to be around other people because I *don't* want to get physical and am therefore *not* into him. There's no way to say that I *am* into him but *don't* want to get physical! Can't I just enjoy a guy's company without all these undercurrents?"

The solution would seem to be straight talk. Yet saying outright, "I really like you, but I don't want to…" may be interpreted as part of the game. (as it often is) A man may assume, "Okay—she's playing 'try and change my mind'." A woman may assume, "Okay—he's playing 'let's see if I can lower her defenses'." Up-front statements are rarely taken seriously.

As a friend once told me, "The nicest thing a guy ever said to me on a date was, 'I want you to know, I don't have any expectations about where this will lead—I just enjoy being with you.' But I didn't believe him."

The bottom line is, the only way to cut out game playing is to cut out the possibility of getting physical. Only then can you accomplish the most important step in forming a relationship and, at the same time, enjoy one of life's greatest pleasures: really getting to know someone.

 ## Fooling Yourself: The Instant Love Game

Our own minds also play games with us. I once spoke to a group of high school kids about holding off on physical relationships.

"Someone define love," I said.

They looked at each other, looked at me, and shrugged.

"Tell you what," I offered. "I'll define it, and you raise your hands if you agree. "Love is…"—my voice took on a dreamy quality—"that feeling you get when you meet the right person."

Every hand went up. And I thought, *Uh-oh.*

Teenagers aren't the only ones who think this way. I recall once randomly picking up a New Age magazine and coming across the same idea—that love is something mysterious and elusive, presumably triggered by a special someone—but stated in far more lofty language.

"Love cannot be defined," it expounded. "One cannot learn to love, for love is found beyond learning. All one can do is remove the obstacles. Love is found in the singular realm of experience."

This is how many people, both young and old, approach relationships. They believe love is an indescribable sensation that is magically and spontaneously generated when Mr. or Ms. Right appears. Just as easily, it can spontaneously *de*generate when the magic "just isn't there anymore." Love streams into your "singular realm of experience," and it can stream out. You fall in love and you can fall out of love.

In my humble opinion, this understanding of love won't get you anywhere. Besides being utter nonsense, it's dangerously mistaken.

First, for love to have real value, the type we yearn for, it has to mean more than a feeling. Feelings alone can't establish a lasting bond. While physical attraction and chemistry feel great and add excitement to a relationship, they can also unconsciously attract you to a lousy human being, a grown-up baby, an abuser, or someone just totally wrong for you.

> *While physical attraction and chemistry feel great and add excitement to a relationship, they can also unconsciously attract you to a lousy human being,*

Yet you won't see this. When people are "high" on love, they block out reality.[1] Their brains become irrational, sharing circuitry with states of mania, intoxication, and obsession[2]—in the words of a leading neuropsychiatrist, similar to "the drug addict desperately craving the next fix."[3]

Furthermore, this over-charged brain state (characterized by elevated levels of the hormone dopamine)[4] can't last more than a year or two, and then illusions give way to reality. Even before this time elapses, love may wane. After all, if love is just a feeling, feelings are fickle; they can be here today, gone tomorrow.

Love, therefore, must be based on something more solid than just attraction and emotion: *reason*. Indeed, while Judaism recognizes the importance and validity of feelings, it places a strong emphasis on the mind. Before losing your heart, you must use your *head* to delve deeply into who your partner actually is. Does he or she have not only a great personality, but also a great *character* and great *values*? In other words, besides being attractive, smart, funny, etc., is he or she kind, caring, giving, loyal, honest, trustworthy, ethical, responsible, and committed? Is he or she growth-oriented and willing to work things out? Will he or she help you become a better person? These are the kinds of qualities that matter in someone with whom you hope to share your life. You must know him or her well enough to know they're there. Playing mind-games with yourself about what love is, in which you allow your emotions to take over, is downright counter-productive.

*Wait a minute! What you're saying sounds right, but doesn't "cherishing touch" conflict with human nature? In any case, isn't it impossible in our society?*

Every human being experiences a lifelong, internal battle between two great drives: the urge for immediate gratification and the desire for far greater pleasure in the long run—the kind that God, in His infinite goodness, designed for us. Embarrassing as the admission may be, which side wins—and the depth of happiness we consequently experience—usually boils down to one thing: maturity.

After I'd presented all the practical reasons for cherishing touch at a local college program, a twenty-one year old student raised his hand.

"Okay, everything you've said makes sense," he conceded, a challenging grin on his face. "But, I mean, like—hey, come on, isn't it just too hard?"

"'Just too hard'?" I countered. "What's going to happen

when you're in law school and have to choose between partying every night or passing the bar? Are you going to shrug off studying with 'it's just too hard'? Cherishing touch isn't an isolated test. Life is full of instances in which you have to delay gratification—and yes, it's hard. But if you don't learn how to do it, you're going to be a big-time loser."

His smile faded.

"There is, of course," I added, "someone I wouldn't call a loser for wanting something and having to have it now." I turned to the group. "Does anyone know who that is?"

No one had a clue.

I turned back to my questioner, who wore a hopeful expression. Looking at him good and hard, I said, "MY TWO-YEAR-OLD!" Whether this student ever got up the guts to change, I don't know, but he got the message.

No, cherishing touch isn't easy. Many things in life aren't. If it's worth it, you do it.

Part of the problem is that we're taught not to expect too much of ourselves—and particularly not of males. This cynicism can be hard to shake. My friend Debbie realized as much when she met a man who planned to reserve all physical involvement for a committed relationship.

"Oh, come on," she said scornfully. "Don't tell me a guy can hold off for that long!"

To her amazement, he was insulted. "Do you really think we men are such babies?" he asked. "If I hung out with half-dressed girls, surfed pornographic websites, or even watched R-rated movies, it would probably be very hard. But I don't. I avoid temptation. I keep busy doing things I have to do and things I enjoy, and I don't look for trouble. A man can make life easy or hard for himself. If we want to, believe it or not, we can control ourselves."

In other words, whether you're male or female, *don't underestimate yourself.* If you're clear in your commitment and structure your life intelligently, you'll be surprised what you can do, and with no great suffering. You're stronger than you think. Thousands of young (and not so young) adults in Israel and in Jewish and Christian communities around the world are at any given moment cherishing touch. If they can do it, so can you.

If you are still doubtful, think of other challenges you meet for the sake of future reward. Can you imagine passing up pizza and ice cream to achieve a healthy weight or to fit into a stunning outfit? Working in a tedious job to earn enough to buy a car? Spending most of your time studying in pursuit of your dream career? Not touching is no different: It's all about delaying gratification for a future goal. Undeniably, physical relationships are a big gratification to delay, but if you're serious about getting the best out of life, you can do it.

"But don't humans need touch?" you may ask. Yes, we do, especially for the oxytocin it gives us. Fortunately, male-female involvement isn't the only way to get it. Affectionate physical contact with just about anyone, including pets, provides an oxytocin boost. Interestingly, so does altruism, and even plain old socializing. We get a chemical high just from being connected to others[5]—it doesn't have to be the opposite sex.

## Not All Attention is Equal

"What about all the attention from guys I'll no longer get?" many girls privately wonder. To which I would reply, "What kind of attention do you really want?"

My friend Karen was working in a restaurant when she decided she wanted to stop getting physically involved with the opposite sex. Her male coworkers, many of whom were accustomed to hooking up, didn't know what to make of her. Not only did they understand that she wouldn't sleep with them, but without making a declarative speech, Karen made clear that she didn't welcome even a casual arm draped around her shoulder. They began paying less attention to her—or so she thought.

Eventually Karen left her job. A few weeks later, one of the waitresses called her. "You saw how all the guys we worked with were always starting up with us but not with you? Well, after you quit, no fewer than *seven* of them told me, '*She's* the kind of girl I want to *marry*.' "

We may assume that this way of thinking died out in the '60s, but many men still judge women differently depending upon what life stage they're in. When they're out for fun in college, they may appreciate those who'll play around with them, but as they mature, they value the ones who won't—the "quality" girls. The fact is that *every girl is a quality girl*. Some just don't know it or act it. Girls who do

## Game-Playing

act it by not being willing to get physical may get less superficial attention, but are likely to get more *real* attention.

A middle-aged woman named Heather recounted something touching from her youth that drove this point home:

"I started rethinking relationships when I was sixteen. In my high school, there was a lot of pressure to be part of the boy-girl scene, and I couldn't resist it. I promised myself that I would date only really nice boys, and—here's the big thing—I wouldn't get physical. Of course, when a boy asked me out, I wouldn't tell him this, because he'd probably never heard of such an idea and wouldn't know what to make of it—or me.

> *"Cherishing touch" may be a challenge to our physical natures, but it is deeply in tune with our spiritual natures.*

"At the end of the date, he'd walk me up to my front door and expect a good-night kiss. But I had it all worked out: I'd smile and say, 'Just a minute,' disappear into the house, and reappear with a bag of chocolate chip cookies I'd baked earlier that day, with a ribbon around it and a note attached. In my cutest voice I'd say, 'Can I give you these instead?'

"And you know what?" Heather concluded with a conspiratorial smile. "I always got asked out again."

Either boys really like chocolate chip cookies (and I wonder if the bags had to get bigger from date to date) or the fact that she was thinking of them earlier in the day, and had taken the time to bake them cookies and write a little note, meant more to them than a kiss. Heather found a way to refocus their attention away from physical expectations and onto her personality and essence.

"Cherishing touch" may be a challenge to our physical natures, but it is deeply in tune with our spiritual natures, where our desire for genuine love lies. If you want a real relationship, you have to act in a way that gets you attention not as a potential "score," but for who you really are.

CHAPTER 5

# THE STRONGEST LOVE POTION

## In Love with Me

We have seen how touch can create illusions of closeness that blur your objectivity regarding your partner and your relationship with him or her. Reserving touch for marriage does just the opposite: It creates the space for something real to develop—the kind of relationship God wants you to have—and for you to appreciate that realness. For the sad truth is, much of what people call "real" love today is as far from real as you can get.

Suppose, for example, that I say, "I love chicken." (I don't—as I said, I'm a vegetarian—but let's just suppose.) "Yummy—my mother makes the greatest chicken. It is so tasty, and I just love it." Does that mean I love *the* chicken? Of course not. If I loved the chicken, I wouldn't cut its throat, cook it, and eat it for dinner. I'd build it a house in the back yard, knit sweaters for it for the winter, and snuggle with it at bedtime. So when I say, "I love chicken," what am I really saying? I'm saying that I love the way *I feel* when I eat chicken. Eating chicken gives *me* pleasure. Who's the focus on? Me. Whom do I really love? *Myself.*

Now, let me ask you something. When someone says, "I love you," wouldn't you like to know which type of love he or she means?

Touch feels good (even better than eating chicken). When touch enters a relationship before a deeper bond has developed, the wonderful sensation you experience may seem like love for the other person when, in fact, it is nothing more than loving how wonderful you feel being with him or her—or, put more bluntly, self-love.

A teenager told me about her friend Alisa's struggle. Alisa's boyfriend had decided (wisely, I thought) that rather than investing in a relationship at this time in his life, he needed to devote all of his energies to studying to secure his future. He suggested they stop seeing each other, even though he felt they had the potential to develop a life-long commitment. Alisa was fighting the idea.

"Does Alisa love her boyfriend?" I asked.

"Of course. That's why she can't bear the idea of no longer seeing him," my young acquaintance replied sadly.

"I'm sure this is very hard for her," I sympathized. "But trying to change his mind means Alisa loves herself, not him. If her feelings for him are genuine, she won't want to keep him from doing what he has to do—as painful for her as it may be."

To quote editor and publisher Margaret Anderson, "In real love you want the other person's good. In romantic love you want the other person."[1]

A "love" such as Alisa's cannot last, for it is not based on true concern for the other. This false love phenomenon is also sometimes described as "being in love with love." When it no longer feels so wonderful, or when real life intrudes, the "love" will quickly go down the drain.

Picture yourself as a woman standing in the moonlight with the man of your dreams. There's a long, romantic silence as you gaze adoringly at each other.

Then he stammers, "I…I just have to tell you…"

At long last—the moment you've been waiting for. "Yes?" you answer breathlessly.

"I want you to know…I…I…" Overcome with emotion, he can barely get the words out.

"Yes? Yes?" You feel dizzy. It's coming—what you've been longing to hear.

He takes a deep breath and looks lovingly into your eyes. "I'm so in love with—*love*."

Would you find that gratifying? I doubt it. He's not in love with *you*—he's in love with a feeling, and this romance has conveniently provided it. This is all about him. He may as well have said, "I'm so in love with—*me*." You? You're interchangeable.

*Girls frequently ask me, "When a boy says 'I love you,' how do I know he means it?"*

Girls frequently ask me, "When a boy says 'I love you,' how

do I know he means it?"

I have a standard reply. "Ask him what he loves about you, and then ask yourself if that's who you are."

My young friend Amy asked her intelligent, articulate boyfriend why he loves her, expecting a deep and moving reply. He responded affectionately, "Because you're so cute."

"Because I'm so *cute!*" she retorted. "Then why don't you get a puppy?"

After breaking up with him, she told me, "My ex-boyfriend saw me primarily as an ornament. He wasn't interested in really knowing me." Not only wasn't this love that could last, it wasn't love to begin with.

This pursuit of self-centered "love" fits our self-centered society. If life is essentially about me, then love is just one more way for me to get my needs and desires fulfilled. What most of us really want is a genuine, other-oriented love.

> *If life is essentially about me, then love is just one more way for me to get my needs and desires fulfilled.*

*Are you suggesting that relationship will last best if we shelve our own needs and desires? Are we supposed to be martyrs?*

Getting past yourself doesn't mean sacrificing your own needs and desires on the altar of another. It's simply the only way to develop true love—that then boomerangs back to you. Whenever we focus on another, we end up being the greatest beneficiaries.

I could say more about this, but I'll let Andy do the talking.

## Andy's Story

Andy, a college football player (and Jewish—yes, there are Jewish football players), and I discussed saving touch for marriage. He impressed me as being far more intelligent and sensitive than your stereotypical jock. One afternoon a few weeks later, Andy showed up at my door.

"I feel like I owe you this visit," he began, looking serious, "because something amazing has happened to me during the past two weeks, and it's got to do with what we were talking about."

"This sounds intriguing," I said with a grin. "Let's hear about it."

"First of all," Andy said, "in case I didn't tell you, everything you said about reserving touch for marriage made a lot of sense. Of course, I wasn't exactly ready to put it into practice, but I have to admit I heard the logic in it."

He took a deep breath.

"Anyway, a couple of weeks ago, I happened to meet this girl named Lori. She had become religious a few years ago. She seemed very bright and friendly, and somehow we started talking. I was very impressed with her. We ended up talking for two hours. It was great. We really connected.

"Now, I want to tell you something. I wasn't even interested in this girl at first. To be honest, her looks didn't do much for me. I couldn't even tell what she looked like under the loose-fitting clothes she was wearing. But I really liked her as a person. Because she was religious, there was no physical contact at all. It was weird for me not to be able to touch her even casually—not even a pat on the back—but I respected where she was coming from. Anyway, we got together the next day and spoke some more—for about six hours. About all kinds of stuff. And also the next day. And the day after that.

"Two weeks have gone by now, and we've spent I don't know how many hours together. Saturday night, we stayed up till five o'clock in the morning just talking and being with each other, and still neither of us wanted to stop. All this time, I swear I haven't so much as touched her hand.

"You know," he continued with just the faintest tinge of embarrassment, "I'm not bragging or anything, but I'm considered pretty hot. I've always gone out with a lot of really attractive women, basically whomever I wanted. You should have seen my last girlfriend—she was a knock-out. I probably don't have to tell you that my relationships weren't exactly 'hands off.' I suppose most of them also weren't so deep.

"But now, for the first time, the exact opposite has happened. Like I said, in the beginning, I didn't even find this girl particularly attractive. It was her mind and personality I was taken with. But now, I'm crazy about her looks, too. Here, let me show you a picture I took of her. I carry it with me all the time. Isn't she cute?"

Andy withdrew a photograph from his shirt pocket, gazed at it with feeling, and handed it to me. It featured a smiling girl, average in appearance.

"She's cute," I agreed.

He beamed, glancing at the picture again before returning it to his pocket.

"But that's not the main thing," Andy continued, pausing as if he himself needed a moment to digest the realization he was about to share. "What's really incredible is that I have never respected a woman so much in my life. And I've never felt so much for anyone in such a short time. I can honestly say I love her. I know," he hastened to add, not wanting to lose credibility, "it must be nothing compared to the love you feel after being married for a few years. But still," he said emphatically, leaning forward, "there's no question in my mind that this is not infatuation. It's the real thing. And I still don't know what she looks like under her clothes. And I don't even care."

Wow, I marveled. Another Big-Time Player bites the dust.

"I just wanted to tell you all this," Andy concluded, "because I am blown away. You have something really powerful going here. What do you call it—'cherishing touch'? Well, I'll tell you—this stuff is the strongest love potion around. You should bottle it and sell it."

Welcome to the world of true love, Andy. True love isn't "I love the pleasure I get from you." True love is "I love you because of who you are." This is the nature of an enduring bond between a man and a woman. Since one's essence doesn't usually change or die, neither will the love.

CHAPTER 6

# WHERE'S THE ROMANCE?

## My Fair Lady

Romance, that heady feeling you get with a special someone, is an ageless and universal phenomenon, and one of our most exhilarating experiences. Yet it can take different forms. In our Western world, there's what's known as medieval romance; there's modern romance; and then there's what I call genuine romance. Before even attempting to answer the burning question, "Can Brandon and Brittany 'cherish touch' and still experience true romance?" we have to clarify which kind we're talking about.

Let's look first at the variety that was popular in the Middle Ages:

Take one Knight and one Fair Lady. Knight, like most males, has a distinct desire for beautiful women. The more religious side of his nature, however, dictates that it is noble to love only that which is good and pure (as opposed to that which is merely pleasing to the eye), and that lust alone is a no-no. To satisfy the demands of both his religion and his male psyche, Knight comes up with an ingenious strategy: He'll use his imagination to infuse physical beauty with virtue, and then convince himself that he's attracted to the virtue rather than the beauty. Milky-white skin will translate into purity of the soul, majestic bearing into upright behavior, an elegant walk into inner grace, and so on, until he can irrationally idolize Fair Lady's (totally contrived) spirit.

Knight is left with two knotty problems. First, physically expressing his passion for Fair Lady will rid her of the very purity that justifies it. Second, his fantasy of Fair Lady's physical and spiritual perfection will be shattered if he ever gets close enough to see the pimples under her makeup.

The solution to both problems? "Love from afar." Thus medieval romance is born. A woman is put on a pedestal to be admired but not approached. You could call it unacted-upon, religiously institutionalized infatuation—the key ingredient being an illusory view of one's "beloved."

In Western tradition, then, romance did not always even involve physical closeness. Since chastity and self-restraint no longer rank among the ten top virtues, "love from afar" has lost its appeal. Now, when two people cook up a romance, they usually season it with a healthy measure of physical intimacy—hence the popular modern version of romance.

## Modern Romance

Physical romance is what most of us dream about and pursue today. Yet it's a complicated business, since being too close for too long eventually destroys all the mystery that provides fertile ground for idealization and illusion. The challenge, therefore, is to include just enough physical intimacy to fan the flames of passion without extinguishing them. Unfortunately, it's difficult to pull this off while living your lives together. You'll soon realize that your relationship stands a better chance of surviving if you restrict it to weekends or even once-a-month rendezvous. You'll also want to create the sensation of escaping the mundane, stress-filled, everyday world and entering an enchanted realm. Among the preferred activities are candlelit dinners (with physical imperfections fading into the shadows), sunset walks on the beach, midnight strolls under starry skies, etc. Activities to be avoided include taking out the garbage, changing dirty diapers, mowing the lawn—in short, anything that resembles reality. Modern romance may be great stuff for movies, but in real life, it doesn't work.

> *Modern romance may be great stuff for movies, but in real life, it doesn't work.*

Nonetheless, a small dose of illusion is very good for a relationship—once the relationship is a done deal.

When can you get "romantic"? Once you're engaged. Once the two of you have decided to spend the rest of your lives together, there's no longer any need to see each other so objectively. I'm not saying you should disregard one another's imperfections—after all, part of your job once you're married will be to help your partner grow into the best person he or she can become, and that requires some awareness of his or her faults. But there's no longer any point in dwelling on them. This is the mate you have chosen and desire. Now is the time to revel in the positive. Be utterly subjective. Delight in what is beautiful about the person you'll be marrying. Let yourself be starry-eyed. There's nothing unhealthy about feeling that your future spouse is the most incredible human being on earth.

## Married Romance

How about once you're married? While you probably won't have to change dirty diapers right away, you will have to deal with garbage that needs taking out, bills that need paying, and adjusting to in-laws. Now you get to reap one of the major rewards of delaying physical contact until after marriage. The excitement created by touch will give your romance an additional major boost that counteracts the real-life challenges you face. It will add a touch of romance because it is new and wondrous. Having chosen the right person for the right reasons, idealizing him or her *now* through the "positive illusions" touch brings about is one of the great keys to marital success.[1] There's nothing wrong with feeling that your spouse is the most incredible human being on earth.

As a healthy marriage progresses, romance stays important. It is vital to find time for the moonlight walks on the beach or the dozen roses on the pillow. However, unlike both classical and modern romance, this married romance is no fantasy. On the contrary, its very reality makes it even more wonderful.

It is quite simply, romance without regrets. It is grounded in the powerful awareness that the two of you have chosen to unite for life, based not upon rose-colored illusions but upon having seen enough of the good (and even the not-so-good) in each other to know, understand and appreciate who one another really is. You are accepting the other person in his or her entirety. That's *genuine* romance, based in committed love. No feeling is more all-encompassing, more joyful—or more real. Physical closeness becomes one of the most wonderful ways to express this passionate love.

Yet even when physical closeness isn't available, the connection stands on its own. It can also be sensed by any observer who's even the tiniest bit tuned in.

Several years ago, Israeli filmmakers made a movie called *Ushpizin* (Aramaic for the "guests" welcomed into one's *sukkah*, the small hut in which Jews eat and sleep during the Feast of Tabernacles). It focused on the lives of an impoverished, childless, religious couple in Jerusalem. Remarkable for most movies involving love—and although the starring actors were married to each other—husband and wife never touched on screen. Israeli movie reviewers commented on this, for it was a revelation for them that, with no displays of physical affection, a couple's love could still come through so powerfully. But it can. This shouldn't be surprising, because if the love is real, physical closeness never determined it to begin with.

Non-physical romance is a great way to focus on the most attractive aspects of the person to whom you're engaged. Physical romance is an even better way to focus on the most attractive aspects of the person to whom you're married. Best of all is when your desire for each other is fueled by genuine romance—the kind developed in the absence of touch, the kind that's real.

Genuine romance is what Andy meant when he called cherishing touch "the most powerful love potion." In the end, nothing beats reality.

*Don't you believe in love at first sight? How do you define love, anyway?*

People can definitely experience attraction at first sight. They can even sense the possibility of a real connection at first sight. But, as I wrote earlier, love means using not only your heart but your *head* to identify positive, admirable attributes in another. *Love stems from knowledge.* "Love at first sight," then, is a contradiction in terms. You can't know someone at first sight.

So love is based in knowledge. Of course, it requires more than that. Once you have decided this is "it," love means intentionally focusing on all the good you see. It's up to you whether to magnify your partner's best or worst traits, and since emotions often result from thoughts, what you think will significantly affect what you feel. If you think beautiful, your love will feel beautiful.

Because love isn't just a feeling, but a conscious appreciation of real qualities, we needn't passively wait for it to happen. We can make it happen. Judaism is a religion of action. Deeds are what count. Love isn't only something we feel, but must be something we *do*. In expressing care, respect and affection for a person in whom we see true beauty, we draw closer to him or her, and *we create love.*[2]

Above all, creating love means giving unconditionally. We tend to think that if we love someone, we'll be moved to give to him or her. The truth, says the great 20th-century ethicist Rabbi Eliyahu Dessler, is the opposite: it is giving that moves us to love.³ This is because we love that which we nurture, that which we've invested in. Indeed, the Hebrew word for love, *ahavah*, contains within it the word "give," *hav*.

> *Love isn't only something we feel, but must be something we <u>do</u>.*

The Psalmist says, "The world is built on kindness"⁴—for the world is about human relationships. We may not want to admit it, but rather than some mystical force, "bigger than both of us," *love is a choice*, something we build by choosing to be kind and loving toward another.

A married woman once shared the following with me. "A relationship has its ups and downs. When you're in a down, you have three choices: Leave, stay in a loveless marriage, or choose to love your spouse. I've always made the latter choice, and in so doing, I've regenerated our love—and that's why I'm still happily married."

Because love stems from acting lovingly, it also *means* acting lovingly. The author of a book on avoiding controlling, abusive relationships writes that if someone mistreats you while professing to love you, remember that *love is a behavior*.⁵

If love is not only emotional but also rational, and if it's not passive but active, then it follows that love has less to do with finding the right person than with *being* the right person. More than seeking out your soul mate, you must become someone capable of being a soul mate to another. For love to work, Judaism says, you must work on yourself—and continue to for the duration of your relationship.

So let me share my own definition of love: *Love is the emotional attachment that results from deeply appreciating, in thought and deed, another's goodness.* Love is loving another's essence, the deepest level of that person's being. This means loving not just his or her looks or even personality, but his or her *soul*—the spark of God within. Only a relationship based on appreciation of the other's goodness will survive the "in love" stage and metamorphose into long-term attachment, and only if you choose to build that soul love through loving actions over a lifetime.

A couple who've achieved this deep connection won't throw in the towel if their relationship takes a downturn. Instead, they'll say, "Underneath it all, you're still the same wonderful person you've always been. If some of the good feelings have gone, we'll have to get them back—and we can, because the basis of our relationship is still solid. No matter what we're going through, I still love you."

This is real love—the love that lasts.

CHAPTER 7

# GOING FOR THE BEST

## Preserving Specialness

I remember an interesting conversation I had back when I was single. It was with Rick, a twenty-four year old who, to put it mildly, did not have a highly spiritual lifestyle or very deep relationships with women. Yet for everything I found distasteful about him (and everything he thought was weird about me, like my pursuit of a meaningful life), we always connected intellectually and often got into intense discussions.

On this occasion, the topic was physical relationships. Rick simply could not understand how people could be willing not to touch. It was absurd. It was against human nature. If I believed in this, I must be off my rocker.

"Rick," I interrupted, "let me ask you something. Have you ever had a purely platonic relationship with a woman that only much later turned romantic?"

He thought for a moment. "Yeah," he said. "Once."

"Well," I continued, "the first time it got physical, didn't it feel different from being with other women? Didn't it mean a lot more?"

There was a pause at the other end of the line.

"Yeah," he conceded slowly. "It did."

"Well," I said, "I'll be doing the same thing. But because I'll be taking it even further, I'm going to get even more out of it."

More silence. I felt I had touched something (figuratively speaking).

"Okay, I get it," he said.

Don't we all want to get the most out of relationships? We want to get the most out of all of life. Indeed, Judaism teaches that God created the world for our pleasure, and created us as pleasure-seekers. We just have to learn how to define pleasure in order to get the most of it. In that vein, the majority of people would probably agree with me that "most" has to do with quality, not quantity; with depth, not breadth. In other words, most people really want not the most out of life but the *best*. They would pass up numerous average enjoyments in favor of a few deep ones. Nowhere is this truer than in relationships. Beneath it all, most sensitive individuals want one lifelong partner with whom they can feel the intense pleasure of uniqueness and singularity that is called "specialness."

God wants all our relationships to be special, but the very first bond he focuses on in Scripture is one man and one woman, married to each other. Ancient Jewish wisdom speaks of God erecting Adam and Eve's wedding canopy and escorting Eve to it.[1] In establishing His world, marriage is the primary relationship.

True specialness results when two people experience something together that neither has experienced before. Of course, specialness begins with emotion. The more exclusive your feelings toward each other, the more powerful they will be. But there's more. If you have known physicality only with each other, that specialness can't be topped. How amazingly, incredibly mind-blowing it is when touch enters your relationship only once you look into each other's eyes as husband and wife.

> *True specialness results when two people experience something together that neither has experienced before.*

## A Unique Moment

Jewish weddings are indescribably moving—especially when they take place in Jerusalem. The ceremony is often outdoors, under the stars. As bride and groom stand beneath a wedding canopy, seven ancient blessings are recited over a cup of wine, recalling Adam and Eve in the Garden of Eden. The blessings praise God for creating joy and peace, and express the hope that we will soon see weddings in the cities of Judah—a fervent prayer that, after long years of exile, we see being answered in front of our eyes. It's hard not to cry.

For the couple themselves, the most romantic part of the Jewish wedding occurs after the ceremony is over. As the crowd bursts into song, the bride and groom take hands—for the first time. (A good videographer will zoom on this.) Singing and dancing, the guests lead them to a room known as the *yichud* room. *Yichud* means seclusion. Until an observant Jewish couple is married, they take care not to be alone together in an isolated place or behind locked doors. Now, as husband and wife, they can be—for the first time. They enter the room, close and lock the door behind themselves, and while the guests move on to the reception room, the couple is granted utter privacy. Since a couple's wedding day serves as a personal Yom Kippur (Day of Atonement) for them, ripe with the opportunity for repentance and starting over, the bride and groom have been fasting up until this point. While the *yichud* room has food and drink to break their fast, I doubt eating or drinking is the first thing on most couples' minds. For here, the new husband and wife can finally hug, kiss and hold one another—for the first time. Most people will probably confess that the *yichud* room was the undisputed high point of their wedding. Only after they bask in each other's company for a while does the newly married couple rejoin their guests to be swept up in exuberant dancing.

I'll never forget something a Jewish woman in her thirties once told me. Rachel had a typical secular social life before deciding to become religious in her last year of college. Shortly afterwards, she met the man she wanted to marry. Throughout their engagement, she and her husband-to-be strictly adhered to Jewish law, and the first time they touched was in the *yichud* room. As a young single, relatively new to observance myself, I was very curious about this. I asked Rachel what it had been like to finally touch the man with whom she would be spending the rest of her life—and, if she didn't mind me asking (I mean, of course it was none of my business, but still...), what did they do in there anyway?

Rachel grinned at the question and blushed but was happy to respond (as I'd figured she would be).

"Well," she said, smiling, obviously savoring the memory from over fifteen years earlier, "I can't speak for other people. I imagine they probably can't wait to hug and kiss each other. For us, the feeling was so intense that neither of us felt the need to do that—at least not right away. For a long time, we stood there, gazing at each other, just holding hands."

I looked at her incredulously. You wait however many months to touch the person you're marrying, and then, when that moment comes, you stand there just holding hands?

Once my shock subsided, I understood—that simple touch was so amazing because it was the first time both Rachel and her husband had ever felt so much for anyone. How unbelievably, incredibly special. Suddenly, I knew how much they each must have wished, thinking back on that day—and especially on their wedding night: "If only *everything* were the first time...."

## Only One First Time

*What you're saying makes sense if you are talking about having relationship after relationship. My boyfriend and*

*I are planning on getting married one day. What's wrong with getting physical if you know that what you have is the real thing?*

Many people delude themselves into believing that the first person with whom they're physically involved is "the one." Unfortunately, real life doesn't bear out such fantasies. One rabbi I know has officiated at twenty weddings in which the bride was not a virgin. The number in which she was marrying the young man with whom she'd lost her virginity was exactly ONE.

Face it: Most relationships don't last. At the same time, we all want specialness. Yet even something earthshakingly wonderful in your first romance relationship will feel more commonplace a few people down the line. With each involvement, your sensitivity is dulled. (More about this ahead.) As a result, that ultimate connection will be less special. So why do people enter so completely into dating relationships, including physically, chipping away at the potential for later experiencing that highest "high" of all?

> *Many people delude themselves into believing that the first person with whom they're physically involved is "the one." Unfortunately, real life doesn't bear out such fantasies.*

The answers are many. First, many people probably reach their deathbeds without ever pondering what the best in life is, never mind the path that will get them there. Second, even a thinking person most likely won't consider an option that seems too "out there," no matter how much sense it may make. Third, even if he or she would contemplate such an option, society doesn't make it easy to swim upstream. Pressure to be "normal," whatever (and no matter how crazy) the current definition happens to be, is almost impossible to combat. As a result, many people have their first—and not especially moving—sexual encounter not because "it was the right person," but because, as someone once told me with a shrug, "it was time." Finally, and most obviously, not everyone self-confident enough to be different can simply listen to his or her brain and resist the enormously powerful urge to get physical—even when the gratification is miniscule compared to the far deeper pleasure he or she may be sacrificing in the long run. Even when that pleasure is what God, who loves us more than anyone else possibly could, wants for us.

"Winning" in life, therefore, requires a clear understanding of your goal, a strategy for achieving it, the courage of your convictions, self-discipline—and, of course, prayer. Armed with these strengths, in addition to a single-minded desire for the best in life, you wouldn't compromise. You wouldn't just say, "What the heck? I'll fool around now and forfeit some specialness with the person I'll be spending the rest of my life with. Whatever's left will have to do."

Those who cherish touch aren't alone in advocating the pursuit of life's deepest pleasures. What makes them different is that they don't just pay lip service to this ideal ("Well, yeah, I guess I do want things to be special, but..."). They actually do it. They understand that saying no many times makes it so much more meaningful when they're ready to say yes.

CHAPTER 8

# THE EXPERIENCE MYTH

## All Experience Is Not Equal

People are often led into casual physical relationships by an unconscious worship of Experience. In a relatively wholesome society, this attitude may mean seeing some degree of physical involvement before marriage as essential to personal growth and development. In the world at large, many take the Experience Principle to the extreme, assuming that the more they sample anything and everything life has to offer, the more enriched they become. Inexperience is equated with losing out. The fact is, there's a lot more to be said for remaining innocent.

I know innocence hasn't been touted as a virtue for some time now. Particularly for secular teenagers, popularity and innocence generally don't go hand in hand. I remember back in 10th grade, a "test" was circulated in which you scored points for your lack of innocence in sexual activity, drug use, and so on, starting one step up from infant-like inexperience and progressing to the dizzying heights of really mature, glamorously self-destructive behavior. The scoring went something like this:

    0-5 = pure as the driven snow
            (an insufferable embarrassment)

    6-10 = still a babe in arms

    11-20 = losing your naïveté

    21-30 = on your way to getting messed up

    31-50 = messed up

    Over 50 = (the coveted) really messed up.

Some people scored so low that they secretly added on ten to twenty points so they could report a respectable total. Meanwhile, those who could get away with it were nonchalantly awarding themselves "75s," and still others were boasting scores that I doubt even the entire Woodstock festival could have matched.

Admittedly, the intensity of such juvenile claims to "sophistication" fades after adolescence. And today, with the appearance of such cheerful phenomena as the AIDS and STD epidemics, as well as widespread substance addiction, some trends have even begun to reverse themselves, to the point where conservatism can be socially acceptable (as long as you're still "cool"). Still, while certain vices are no longer glorified, the mystique of worldliness lingers. Experience remains the name of the game.

Obviously, to live is to experience. Yet I would urge that experimentation not take place indiscriminately and for its own sake. Experiencing should be a highly selective means to a lofty end: becoming a better, more sensitive, and ultimately happier person. Far too often, however, the only result is pain and emotional damage. As American writer Minna Antrim famously wrote, "Experience is a good teacher, but she sends in terrific bills."[1]

What's worse, we don't always possess the wisdom to learn what we should from our experiences. Following a breakup, you may learn where you need to grow, or only where your ex does. You may learn why you keep attracting the wrong people, or why others can't be trusted. You may learn how to achieve love, or that it's an impossible dream. Experience alone guarantees nothing.

Some years ago, I spoke with a single professional hardened by years of failed physical relationships. "Experience has taught me to stop hoping," she informed me flatly. "I've learned to become so independent that I don't even care if there's a man in my life." Yet what she'd "learned" only made her less likely to get the love for which she still yearned, deep beneath her pain and denial. Experience may be educational, but education doesn't always equate with wisdom.

Unfortunately, the temptation to "broaden" oneself through some hopefully harmless experience remains alluring, and many fall for it. Do yourself a big favor. Don't get sucked in.

## The Power of Hindsight

If you still have doubts, ask a few sensitive and sincere people in committed relationships—or better yet, a few newlyweds—whether, if given the chance to live their lives over, they would change anything. I've watched many people grow, from their first date with their spouse-to-be until a few years have passed and they are part of an "old, settled, married couple," and I've seen a similar evolution of thought among most of them, culminating in an almost universal conclusion.

When people are very new to a relationship, they'll often say, "I'm glad I met this person at this time in my life and not earlier. I wouldn't want to have missed many of the things I've done up until now. I wouldn't trade those great experiences for anything."

However, as time goes on, people's perspectives on the past often changes somewhat. They'll say, "I wish I hadn't done everything I did before finding the right person. I mean, I did gain from some of my experiences, and I probably have an understanding and appreciation of relationships that I might not have otherwise. But it would have been nicer if I could have learned what I did with my current love and skipped all that stuff."

Later still, particularly after they're married for a few years, the refrain often evolves into something entirely different. "Ugh, when I think of some of the things I did before getting married! It was so stupid. I would give anything to have had my husband/wife be my only relationship. Hopefully my kids won't have to go through what I did." (Too bad only hindsight is 20/20.)

Why are these anti-Experience feelings so strong? First and foremost, there's the big, big issue of forfeited sensitivity and singularity, as we've discussed. Each previous involvement lingering in one's memory dilutes the specialness with one's husband or wife that most of us intensely desire.

I once spoke with someone who felt this loss more acutely than anyone I'd ever met.

"I consider myself a good, religious girl," she began, "and I've never touched a boy. This year I started dating. A few weeks ago, I started going out with a boy who's very nice, but not quite as religious as I am. We really like each other, and we've been getting closer. Recently, he started saying that it's getting so hard for him not to touch me. He says he knows I don't want to and respects me for it, but he still really wants to kiss me."

Here it comes, I said to myself.

"Well," she continued, a blush of shame rising to her cheeks, "last week, one evening, we were out walking in a park… and there weren't really any people around…and it felt very romantic…and all of a sudden—he kissed me. And I let him." She looked down in embarrassment.

There was a long pause. When she raised her head again, her face wore a pathetic expression. "And now…" she said sadly, "now…I feel like…used merchandise!"

As her words registered, I had two reactions. "Honey," my pre-religious inner voice replied incredulously, "you feel like 'used merchandise'—and all you did was kiss someone? You must be part of some nearly extinct species!"

At the same time, my present religious personality, the side connected to God and to truth, thought sadly, "Poor girl. She's right." My heart went out to her.

This young woman's words were very precious to me. In a world where everything means so little, she knew she had lost something because her husband would no longer be the first man she'd kiss. Some people may think this is sweet. Others may think it's ludicrous. I think it's enviable. Because if she's so sensitive to what she's lost, then once she's married, she's going to be just as sensitive to everything she has. That's something to which, in my opinion, "experience" can't hold a candle.

> *As important as it is to be <u>objective</u> when you're dating, <u>subjectivity</u> is what it's all about once you've found the right one.*

## And the Winner Is...

Another source of disenchantment with the Experience Principle is the unpleasant tendency toward comparisons. As important as it is to be *objective* when you're dating, *subjectivity* is what it's all about once you've found the right one. Ideally, you'll want to feel that no one can possibly measure up to your unbelievably wonderful partner. Yet each physical involvement opens the door wider to innumerable comparisons between him or her and some previous boyfriend, girlfriend, or hookup. Needless to say (since your partner will probably not compare favorably in *every* respect, no matter how fabulous he or she is), such evaluations don't do either one of you—or your relationship—any good.

The truth is, subjectivity can be destroyed even when we *look at* others. Research has found that married men shown photos of stereotypically beautiful women found their wives less attractive and felt less committed to their marriages.[2] Another group of married men who looked at revealing photos of models later described themselves as less in love with their wives.[3] Can you imagine how much more negatively impacted might they be were they to have slept with these women?

My friend Carol, a speaker on relationships and marriage, shared with me a remark made by one audience member at a public talk she gave. Carol had pointed out that the absence of past partners with whom to compare your spouse strengthens your marriage, while memories can make for problems. Immediately a man (whose wife I assume was not present) volunteered (and publicly, no less) the following delightful comment:

"I know what you mean. I've been married for two years, and I really love my wife, but—especially in our most intimate moments—I can't help thinking about my previous girlfriend, who was better."

When Carol told me that, I cringed. If I were that man's wife and overheard what he said, I'd be devastated. Every time I quote him in my own talks, looks I get from the participants indicate that I'm not alone. The nearly unanimous reaction is UGH. (The people who don't respond with "ugh" usually look distinctly uncomfortable, apparently having been in a situation where they thought something along the same lines as this man.)

A quote from ancient Jewish wisdom brutally sums up this unpleasant reality. "When a divorced man marries a divorced woman," it states, "there are four minds in the bed." In other words, each partner drags in memories of his or her previous spouse. If that doesn't sting enough, the quote adds, "not all fingers are alike"—that a woman may make even the most intimate comparisons between her current and previous husbands. ("Fingers" is a euphemism.)[4]

Females, in fact, are at the greatest risk for having such thoughts intrude into their current relationship. The part of the brain responsible for memory, the hippocampus, is larger and more active in women than in men. Furthermore, the hippocampus attaches feelings to memories. A woman is thus more likely than a man is to remember not just the facts of an event, but also how it felt emotionally.[5] The upshot is that a woman's past can be nearly as real to her as her present is.

Unfortunately, neither women nor men recognize the lifelong impact of their experience. An eighteen-year-old male once demonstrated this shortsightedness:

"I have a two-stage approach to relationships," he explained. "Stage One is, I'm eighteen and not thinking about anything serious, so I'm going to have fun—if you know what I mean. Stage Two will be when I'm older and ready to settle down. Then I'll clean up my act. I'll find a girl who was never into hooking up, we won't touch, and I'll reap all the benefits you talk about. In other words," he concluded triumphantly, "I'm going to 'have my cake and eat it, too'!"

When I presented this philosophy to a group of young women, they were incensed. "What kind of garbage is that?" they demanded. "He gets some nice girl, and she gets some guy who's been everywhere? That's not fair!"

Before they could march out and burn this guy in effigy, I told them how I had responded. For his outlook wasn't just "unfair." This young man was completely unaware of the utter fallacy in his "best of both worlds" logic.

"Forgive me for bursting your bubble," I had told him, "but you don't realize that when you get to Stage Two, you'll no longer be the person you would have been without Stage One. You're going to enter marriage with a storehouse of memories, comparisons and a grossly eroded sensitivity. Now that you've 'had your cake,' it won't be there to 'eat' anymore. There's no going back. You've blown it. Get it?"

In short, his approach may have cheated the woman he would someday marry, but he was being just as unfair to himself.

The truth is, once they find their soul mate, most people don't exactly relish their memories of past physical encounters. Nonetheless, such recollections stick with you, surfacing when you least want them to. Someone I know likened them to flies persistently buzzing around your head. Sometimes the thought of having been physically involved with a particular person can be overwhelmingly embarrassing. Probably most happily married individuals would be grateful if their past relationships, good and bad alike, could be erased with a wave of their hand. One woman even told me, quite seriously, that if some brain surgeon could remove all her memories of anyone but her husband, she'd go for it. In the meantime, she said, all she can do is pray that God makes them disappear.

*What you're saying is fine for young people who grew up understanding this system and followed it. Is there any comfort for those of us who made poor choices in the past, but now see the wisdom of cherishing touch?*

I want to interject something important. Some people—particularly females—who regret past behaviors feel that if they've already had some physical or sexual involvement, they're "ruined," and there's no hope for them. They couldn't be more wrong. If that were so, it would discourage us from growing as we move through life.

God is the God of Second Chances (and Third, and Fourth, and Fifth…). While we cannot undo the past and must face the consequences of our actions, we can (in ways we don't always understand) redeem the past by sincerely changing our ways. Both the Bible and history are replete with examples of those who became great as a *reaction* to terrible wrongs they committed. Jews see Jacob's fourth son, Judah, as a prototype of sinning and repenting, and for this overcoming of the past, the kings of Israel descend from him. Clergyman John Newton's slave trading past led him to be a powerful anti-slavery voice as well as an inspiration to millions through his song *Amazing Grace*. Certainly, those of us who have made personal errors can also transcend those mistakes. Myriad examples like these can show how a negative experience can catapult us higher than we might have reached without it.

In Jewish tradition, each lunar month is associated with one of the signs of the zodiac. The time of year particularly suited to starting over occurs during the month of Elul (usually falling out over the period of August and September), which precedes Rosh HaShanah, the Jewish New Year. What is incredible is that the astrological sign for this month is a virgin. This is to remind us that we can never be irrevocably defiled. In the physical world, we may not be able to restore virginity, but in the spiritual world, we can. No matter what we've done or what has happened to us, a place in our souls remains pure. At any time and however far down a wrong path we may think we are, we can always tap into that place.

Those who have made mistakes, in fact, have a unique opportunity. Ancient Jewish wisdom states: "In the place where the repentant stand, even the perfectly righteous cannot stand."[6] This is not meant to encourage us to do wrong or foolish things, but it does make us aware that, *after the fact*, there are benefits in which we can take comfort. As someone who lived a secular lifestyle until age twenty-two, I have a far greater personal appreciation of sexual morality than I would otherwise have, and I am immensely grate-

> *In short, you are never "ruined." You can always return, stronger than before.*

ful for that. My previous mistakes have, in their own way, brought me closer to God and increased my love for Him.

In short, you are never "ruined." You can always return, stronger than before. You are always God's beloved child. Knowing that goes a long way in helping you to overcome the drawbacks in human relationships that result from past behavior.

Even those with no relationship with God recognize the universality of "turning over a new leaf." Life would be oppressive and dark if we didn't accept that, despite all our mistakes, each day brings new opportunity. This book is meant as a path forward, not as a weight to cause anyone to feel burdened by past behavior.

Nevertheless, the mistake in thinking that cherishing touch means "missing out" should be clear. You're not missing out by not doing something now if later you'll be relieved you didn't do it. When you're happily settled down with your partner for life, you won't regret all those "experiences" you missed. You'll know with certainty that the only thing you've missed is what lies ahead.

CHAPTER 9

## A HEART IN ONE PIECE

## Sparing Yourself Pain

Human beings are exceedingly vulnerable. One fall on our face and we may need stitches. One wrong turn on our skis and we may find ourselves with a broken leg. Thankfully, God gave our bodies the ability to heal, but even with proper medical attention, we may end up scarred or disabled.

One of the most amazing messages of ancient Jewish wisdom is that God created physical reality as a manifestation of a deeper spiritual reality. The physical and spiritual worlds parallel each other. For example, God created women to be more tuned in to the value of privacy. Even among other females, girls usually won't strip down entirely to go swimming, whereas boys will. (In fact, my father told me that his high school boys' swim team used to practice naked. The girls' team, needless to say, didn't.) That women have greater spiritual sensitivity to privacy and men have less is reflected in our bodies: the female reproductive organs are internal, whereas male reproductive organs are external.

Similarly, our physical vulnerability reflects a deeper

spiritual vulnerability. Childhood traumas may reverberate throughout our adult lives, and even smaller hurts may take months to fade. As fragile as we are physically, we are often even more so emotionally.

> *As fragile as we are physically, we are often even more so emotionally.*

Once, as I introduced myself as a speaker to a group of young adults, I noticed a deadly serious look on the face of one woman in the room. I began by saying that I wanted to talk about how to avoid emotional investment in a doomed relationship. The woman sat back in her chair, arms folded, wearing a tight, pained expression. I gave an example of a dead-end relationship, in which only one partner sought a long-term commitment. Her face darkened and she nodded almost imperceptibly. "Hmm," I thought. "Seems like this must have happened to her." I gave a second example, that of a relationship that eventually and painfully terminated because the partners' life goals did not coincide. She looked even more miserable, sighed heavily and nodded again, this time quite visibly. "Oh no," I thought, "this, too?" I felt hesitant about continuing, but didn't have much choice. I took a deep breath and gave my final example: an unhealthy relationship. I wasn't prepared for what happened next. Her eyes filled with tears, she got up, and walked out.

This woman was in considerable pain. Had her suffering been physical, she probably would have been hospitalized. Then again, had she anticipated such great physical distress, she would have, from the beginning, been much more cautious.

Most of us—particularly females—are quite wary of physical risks. We will not, for example, jump off a diving board without knowing if there is water in the pool below. Feelings, on the other hand, are intangible. Emotional dangers are therefore far more difficult to identify and take seriously.

The sad truth is that because of the subtlety of emotional damage, countless people throw caution to the winds, dive into empty pools, and then walk around with the equivalent of open wounds and fractured limbs. Women, who are often more emotionally vulnerable, undoubtedly suffer the most—but men can get badly hurt as well. Most of these victims don't even realize the extent of their injuries. Yet one's heart can suffer as surely as one's body. Although time may heal all wounds, the scars remain.

## Expecting Good—or Bad?

Jewish tradition tells us that when a baby is in the womb, an angel stands by its head, teaching it everything there is to know, all the wisdom of this world. Upon being born, the baby forgets everything, and spends its entire time on earth relearning it.[1] Among the priceless things the angel teaches us is that life is good. Some people, thanks to good parenting, relearn this lesson quickly. Others aren't as fortunate. For all of us, much depends on our experiences.

Since relationships are so central to our lives, they largely determine our outlook. When we succeed in a relationship, life looks bright. Every time we are clobbered emotionally, the light dims.

"I feel I left part of myself with my ex-girlfriend," a young man once told me. "Once you give of yourself, you can't just take it back. Now I'm afraid to let that happen again."

Even one break-up can leave you too mistrusting to invest in another relationship. Eventually, hopelessness sets in, leading you to conclude that optimism about life is only for the foolish or blind.

I once had a brief encounter with a very unhappy eighteen-year-old girl. Dawn had been heavily involved with a number of boys who, one after another, had come and gone in her life. When I met her, she had just followed her latest boyfriend to Jerusalem. Shortly after she'd arrived, he'd broken up with her. She was in despair. It pained me to hear her speak.

"I've had it with relationships!" she said tearfully, her shockingly deep bitterness cutting like a knife. "I never want to have anything to do with men again as long as I live."

I'm sure other teenage girls have mouthed similar sentiments after a breakup, but I had never seen such utter disillusionment in a person that young. I felt as if I were listening to a jaded older woman who'd divorced a succession of abusive and unfaithful men. Yet Dawn had barely reached adulthood. Had she grown up in a different environment, she might have retained a positive and trusting perspective on life and relationships. I knew I was witnessing a tragedy that needn't have happened.

If we want not only healthy limbs and organs but also healthy psyches, we have to treat our souls as carefully as our bodies. We have to be just as wary of emotional cliffs as physical ones, and we have to understand how easy it is to step over the edge.

Few areas of life involve greater emotional intensity, and therefore greater risk, than relationships. When you become involved with someone, you let down the self-protective barrier you erect in your dealings with others. You put your emotions on the line. You allow yourself to be vulnerable. Even with physicality out of the picture, you have a lot to lose. Add the powerful bond physical closeness can create, and immeasurably more is at stake.

Each time a relationship ends—or just doesn't pan out—you pay a price. You grow less confident in your ability to distinguish reality from fantasy. You lose faith in the permanence of relationships and the goodness of others. You may lose faith even in the goodness of God. In the end, you forfeit the lesson the angel taught you, the optimism essential to happiness.

> *Each time a relationship ends —or just doesn't pan out— you pay a price.*

This defeat is sad enough. But that isn't the end of the damage. A vicious circle is also set in motion. The next time you meet someone, you are already on your guard. You no longer trust enough to let down your walls. The other person, in turn, may, consciously or unconsciously, sense how emotionally closed you are and back out of the relationship, dealing your trust yet another blow. You then retreat deeper into your protective shell, further dimming the prospect of future success. Disillusionment thus gives rise to fatalism, which becomes a self-fulfilling prophecy.

One of the most effective strategies for not getting hurt is not bonding completely with another person until it is safe to do so. While we must gradually lower our emotional walls, keeping the physical "wall" up until the relationship is assured offers tremendous protection. Cherishing touch helps secure your happiness—and your future.

## No Pain, No Gain?

*Isn't the pain of failed physical relationships essential to growth? Aren't you recommending sheltering people from the real world?*

This question can be asked only if one assumes such a thing as "The Real World," some universal social reality in which, among other things, a certain amount of pain is necessary for optimal personal growth.

In fact, "The Real World" is a subjective concept defined by whatever risks, physical and emotional, a person's own lifestyle entails. If, for example, you come from an upper-middle-class background, you probably regard life in a crime-ridden, inner city slum with horror, while you see a group like the Amish as living in an artificial bubble—your own lifestyle being, of course, the most natural and normal one. However, a ghetto teenager would scorn your existence as no more "real" than that of a baby in a playpen, while the Amish would view your society with the same apprehension with which you view that inner city slum.

Within large parameters, every culture creates its own social reality based on its own values. A culture that values, for instance, sophistication, learning through trial and error, and experiencing emotional pain as the path to maturity will create one kind of existence for its members. A culture that values innocence and sees no point in learning things the hard way will take emotional pain seriously and create a very different kind of existence. The issue is not what constitutes "The Real World," but what any social group wants to constitute *its* real world. Accordingly, the crucial question is not which humanly created existence is more "real," but which is more conducive to emotional health and happiness.

Understanding this idea means we must view pronouncements as to how much and what kinds of pain are necessary in life with skepticism. While you undoubtedly perceive some of what a ghetto teenager has to go through as needless, he or she probably wonders how you'll ever mature in your little cocoon. At the same time, the Amish may well pity you for what your society forces you to endure, while you can't imagine how their cloistered lifestyle doesn't stunt their growth.

We have to ask ourselves why we think that the pain accompanying modern-day life is necessary.

Of course, many people jump to defend the system. "I

would never be the person I am today if I hadn't gotten hurt in life," the refrain usually goes. "Everything I've gone through, I've gained from."

I'm not arguing with the assertion that one (hopefully) learns and grows through suffering. What I am arguing with is the idea that we should therefore deliberately set ourselves up for it. If I were hit by a train and had to spend the next year in a cast from head to toe, I would gain an unmatched understanding and appreciation of the frailty of the human body. That doesn't mean I'm going to go out and stand on the tracks waiting for the 6:30 express.

Anything learned through pain comes at a price: inevitable and sometimes permanent damage to one's body or—far worse—one's heart. In most cases, we cannot foresee what this price will be, or if it's worth paying. Too often, the cost far exceeds the benefit.

For example, I assume that even the most liberal-minded mother wouldn't suggest that her daughter try prostitution as a learning experience. Likewise, upon discovering her daughter already gainfully employed in the field, this mother would not simply sigh, "Well, I guess it is all part of growing up." The utter self-degradation of prostitution overrides any "educational" value it may have.

Obviously, few situations are this clear-cut. That's where we really have to be careful. We've talked about the emotional toll of broken relationships in terms of desensitization and despair. When we get involved in a relationship that seems harmless, but is likely to end, are we wise enough to know we'll emerge the better for it rather than the worse? By separating physicality from the relationship, we are placing a protective barrier around ourselves.

To a mind that cherishes sensitivity and emotional wholeness, many "learning experiences" aren't what they're cracked up to be. They're fun and temporarily gratifying but, in the final analysis, simply not worth it. Cherishing touch shields you from much of the suffering around you. God will make sure you get the pain you need to grow—no more and no less, without you seeking it out.

Advocating saving touch for marriage, therefore, is not overprotective. It's simply more intelligent. This may explain why many smart people are choosing to make the world of "cherishing touch" their real world.

CHAPTER 10

# IT MEANS NOTHING TO ME

## Preventing Desensitization

The best (or worst) part about giving talks on relationships is what participants tell me afterwards. At the conclusion of one talk at a university, I privately asked a girl if the campus social scene was really as casual as I'd heard.

"Probably," she said. "I've hooked up with twenty guys this semester." She didn't even bat an eye.

I mentioned earlier that having repeated casual physical encounters can blunt your sensitivity. Eventually, nothing means anything anymore. Still, I'd always assumed that women, who have a greater oxytocin response, feel some sense of loss, some hurt—*something*—after even a fleeting physical connection. Yet, for some time now, high school and college students have been telling me that not only boys, but also girls, can repeatedly hook up and have no feelings for their partners afterwards.

"That goes totally against female nature," I've argued. "A girl who claims she can do that is either in denial or on Prozac," (which is sometimes prescribed for women who are "overly sensitive" to rejection).[1] Lately, however, I've begun wondering if I'm wrong and if the explanation for this equal-opportunity desensitization could have a chemical basis—rooted in oxytocin.

There are a few theories that link oxytocin to emotional desensitization. One harkens back to early development. Ideally, we learn to produce oxytocin by being cuddled as children, especially in the first three years of life.[2] However, if parents aren't attuned to a baby's needs, or if they're unavailable most of the day and surrogates don't provide enough loving physical attention, a child may never develop a strong oxytocin response. Early deprivation, therefore, may underlie the later phenomenon of getting physical with no emotional bonding.[3]

Theoretically, that could explain the hookup scene: all these kids had inadequate parenting. Yet while some of today's college students undoubtedly lacked a close connection with their parents or were sent to poorly staffed day-care centers, this clearly can't be the whole story.

Another suggestion I've heard has to do with testosterone. Young women are playing more competitive sports than they used to, and it's well known that athletic competition raises testosterone levels, which means a lower oxytocin response. Perhaps the greater number of female "jocks" can account for women's increasingly blasé attitude toward physicality. Yet research doesn't show that only athletes are affected.

One explanation that intrigues me focuses not on the past

and not on aggressive sports, but on the present-day social lives of these young people—and it involves something called neuroplasticity.

## Neuroplasticity

Neuroplasticity means that throughout our lives, our brains grow and change. This is a blessing, as positive adult experiences can help a formerly neglected child learn to produce oxytocin.[4] Yet, like so many of God's gifts, neuroplasticity can be a force for good or for bad. We must ask if *negative* adult experiences can help an otherwise emotionally *healthy* person learn *not* to produce oxytocin.

A doctor once shared the following with me.

"Did you ever wonder what happens to a woman who's gotten physical with too many men? How can she feel connected not just to one guy she's no longer with, but to another, and another, without suffering an emotional breakdown? She probably can't—so her brain steps in to save her. In each subsequent relationship, her brain secretes less oxytocin. She therefore experiences less bonding in the relationship and less pain when it ends. In extreme cases—as with prostitutes—oxytocin activity may cease altogether." In other words, if a woman involves herself with too many men, she can negatively affect her hormonal state.

"The problem is," he continued, "that when such a woman finally meets the right man, her oxytocin levels are on the floor, so she can't forge the same hormonal bond with him as she once could have. She no longer feels what she's supposed to feel."

In other words, there may be a hormonal explanation for the phenomenon one woman in her late thirties described: "If you're so busy turning yourself off, then you can't just turn yourself on when you're with someone you love."[5]

The doctor concluded: "A woman can kill her own oxytocin response."

Could this be true? I did some research, and learned that this theory of decreasing oxytocin—promoted by a leader in the abstinence movement—had created a bit of a furor, causing at least one scientist to slam it as "complete pseudo-science."[6]

I therefore contacted Susan Kuchinskas, author of a book on oxytocin, for her opinion. She said the controversial theory claims that oxytocin can be "used up" in premarital relationships, leaving an inadequate amount for marriage. As she stated, this obviously makes no sense. Take the mother-child relationship: Mothers don't use up their oxytocin on their first child, but remain capable of bonding with however many more children they have.[7] Similarly, research has found that men and women don't use up their oxytocin on their first sexual partner, but remain capable of bonding with subsequent partners.[8]

However, what if that first or even a later relationship ends painfully? Could that pain set off a defense mechanism that inhibits oxytocin production and therefore bonding in

*In male-female relationships, could painful breakups harm bonding with future partners?*

subsequent relationships? With a mother, could painful separation from a child weaken her connection with her future children? In male-female relationships, could painful break-ups harm bonding with future partners?

According to Kuchinskas, the answer may be yes:

> Certainly, neuroplasticity goes both ways. ... Can broken premarital relationships adversely affect the oxytocin response? I think it is possible. Think of the oxytocin response as a habit, a learned response. Certainly habits can be broken or changed. ...
>
> I do think it's likely that the oxytocin response...can change for the worse, as well as for the better. So, I agree with you that painful sex or love experiences as a child, young adult, or even full-grown adult could maybe not destroy but inhibit the oxytocin response.[9]

## Learning Not to Feel

A few examples come to mind that illustrate this possibility. I heard about a Holocaust survivor's daughter born after the war, whose mother was emotionally detached from her. This girl later discovered that, while in a concentration camp, her mother had given birth to a baby who was immediately murdered. The trauma, where bonding with a baby led to unbearable pain, apparently destroyed this woman's ability to connect with her next child.

Similarly, I know a woman who suffered repeated sexual

assault as a young teenager. Having physical and emotional intimacy painfully wrenched apart, she needed help to learn how to experience emotional closeness through sex. This is a common reaction to sexual trauma.

These are both extreme cases. But I don't think it is far-fetched to imagine that a lower level of pain—say, repeated hookups in which the other person doesn't even call afterwards—could inhibit future bonding.

The idea that premarital relationships that terminate painfully (as most do) may impair our oxytocin response is only a theory, and is contested by those who see no harm in current sexual mores. Nevertheless, given the reports I've gotten from college campuses about the utter emotional detachment with which women engage in sexual activity, it makes startling sense to me. I believe we should take it seriously. The more we learn about the brain, the more we know that feelings and hormones are connected. Perhaps, indeed, desensitization is not only emotional but also chemical. If so, this should give us a great deal more appreciation of what God had in mind in asking us to cherish touch.

*If the idea is to avoid desensitization and wait until you've found the right person and made a commitment, why keep waiting until marriage? What's wrong with getting physical once you're engaged?*

If engaged couples had the green light for getting physical, the time between meeting someone and engagement would shrink considerably, and an unprecedented number of engagements would be taking place (and broken engagements, and new engagements, and new broken engagements…). Because of the normal and powerful desire for physical closeness with a member of the opposite sex, men and women would fool themselves into thinking they'd found the right person so they could become engaged and start experiencing those pleasurable feelings already. The subconscious is quite capable of such tricks, and this one is child's play.

"Well, then," you may question, "if you're worried about people getting engaged just to have a physical relationship, isn't there a risk they'll get *married* for the same reason?"

Despite our propensity for self-deception, my response to this question is no. That's because engagement and marriage are very different. Let me illustrate with a story.

When I was a teenager, a woman named Anne lived behind our house. Shortly after she and her husband divorced, I began noticing a man hanging out at her place. One day I saw him in Anne's backyard, shooting baskets. I went up to the fence separating our yard from hers and started chatting with him.

"I've seen you around here a lot lately," I began innocently. "Have you just moved into the neighborhood?"

"Yeah," he answered nonchalantly. "I'm living with Anne."

As a rather naïve sixteen year old, I was a bit taken aback. Not as tuned into privacy as I am now, I asked, "Why don't you guys get married?"

Challenged by my bluntness, he apparently decided to

educate me. "We don't need to get married," he countered, somewhat defensively. "We know we love each other, and we're committed to each other. We don't need a piece of paper to prove it."

He dribbled the ball a couple of times and shot another basket. "Besides," he added, "I'm not ready to get married yet."

Only later did I catch the contradiction: Living together is the same level of commitment as being married, but he's not ready to get married. That's when I realized that somebody was kidding himself.

Just as, deep down, Anne's boyfriend knew that there's a big difference between being married and living together, we all know there's a big difference between being married and being engaged. Marriage entails legally and spiritually joining with another, deepening your commitment immeasurably. The thought of jumping into the wrong marriage and then having to terminate it generates considerable fear, both conscious and unconscious. Divorce inflicts untold emotional pain and scars. As painful as ending a relationship is, ending a marriage is immeasurably more so. Even the cost of a wedding as well as its public nature serves to put the brakes on jumping into marriage. A couple could run off on a romantic whim to the Elvis Chapel in Las Vegas and get hitched, but few couples pick that option.

Engagement, on the other hand, is a verbal agreement that can be easily made and easily broken. While undoubtedly very upsetting, calling off a wedding, particularly early in the planning stages, is not the end of the world. Even closer to the date, when there might be more emotional pain, public embarrassment and financial loss, there's no comparison between terminating the relationship before as opposed to after the ceremony. Never underestimate the power of the subconscious—it is fully aware of this difference.

If all we had to do in order to give our hormones free rein was to get engaged, we'd be far more susceptible to confusing them for "the real thing." Assuming we did fall victim to this deception, we'd scarcely be better off than if we were dating without cherishing touch. We'd face the same risks—sacrifice of objectivity, loss of opportunity for something deeper to develop, a painful breakup, etc.—with the only difference being that we would call ourselves engaged (as opposed to merely "seeing someone") for the downward spiral to begin. If we did make it through engagement to marriage, we'd be just as likely to have married the wrong person based upon an illusion.

## The Marriage Covenant

Even if you're convinced of the wisdom of not touching before marriage, you might encounter one more scenario. Perhaps you didn't begin your relationship thinking, "When we get engaged, we'll get physical." Rather, you fully intended to reserve touch for marriage, and succeeded for a good while, but now that you're engaged, you feel your resolve weakening.

"We've been good," you tell yourself, "and we've reaped the benefits. We've maintained our objectivity and developed the beginning of true love. At this point, would it be so terrible if we started touching?"

As I've discussed, Judaism teaches that the physical was created to express the spiritual. When we say a blessing and express gratitude to God for our food, eating is elevated to a holy act. When we dress in a way that reflects our souls, our bodies become holy. Likewise, when we engage in a physical relationship to express a spiritual bond, touch becomes holy.

The question is, "What determines this spiritual bond?" You might assume love does. Judaism disagrees.

Imagine the following two scenarios:

One: You've been going out with someone for a long time. He or she looks into your eyes and says sincerely, "I love you…but I'm not ready to commit."

Two: You've been going out with someone for not such a long time. He or she looks into your eyes and says sincerely, "It might still be a while before I can unreservedly say 'I love you.' But I know I want to spend the rest of my life with you."

Which scenario moves you more?

As powerful as love is, if it lacks commitment, it's not solid. More importantly, it's not holy. Marriage is a covenant encompassing a man, a woman and God Himself.

> *As powerful as love is, if it lacks commitment, it's not solid. More importantly, it's not holy.*

Within a marriage, physicality is sanctified. Marriage—even if the love is still embryonic— transforms a relationship, including our physical union, into something Godly.

Years ago, when I couldn't imagine marrying someone I didn't at least think I loved, my friend Jamie got engaged to a man she hadn't known for long. I was surprised.

"Do you love each other?" I wanted to know.

"Not yet," Jamie replied.

I was aghast. "But you feel ready to get married?"

"Absolutely. My fiancé is a wonderful person. We totally respect, admire and appreciate each other. We enjoy being together. We have great communication. We share the same values and life goals. And we're physically attracted to each other. We have all the ingredients necessary for love but one: enough time spent together. We could continue going out until we love each other and then get married; or we can go ahead now, knowing that the love will soon be there. If we know it's right," Jamie concluded, "why wait?"

Jamie's story reminds me of the Biblical story of Isaac and Rebecca. All Isaac knew about his wife-to-be was that Eliezer, his father Abraham's faithful servant, had chosen her, and that both Eliezer's closeness to Abraham and Abraham's blessing ensured that Rebecca was a wonderful match for him. The Biblical verse about their marriage is striking. It tells us that Isaac married this special girl, and *afterwards* he loved her.[10] Love doesn't always lead to commitment, but commitment nearly always leads to love. Yet even before the love came, their commitment to each other sanctified their physical relationship. So too with couples like Jamie and her husband.

One little-discussed problem with premarital physical relationships is that, upon marrying, you must flip a mental switch and perceive something that may have originally been merely fun, exciting or lustful as *holy*. A friend of mine, who was physically involved with her boyfriend before they both became religious and decided to marry, sensed the need for this change. As the wedding approached, she begged him, "Please make our wedding night be different." According to at least one sex therapist who counsels newlywed couples, those who can't make this transition may shut down sexually. How sad when we have trouble seeing sexuality as the beautiful expression of spiritual commitment it is.

A couple may deeply love each other and think they're soul mates, but until they marry, they are spiritually separate. Since the physical is meant to express the spiritual, they must remain physically separate as well. When they are finally pronounced husband and wife and enter a holy, spiritual union, their souls finally "touch"—and so can their bodies.

In short, engagement is not a definitive commitment, but merely a "'commitment' to [later] be committed." Only marriage itself, a true and total commitment permeating all levels of the conscious and subconscious, can provide the optimal framework for experiencing touch with fewer risks, greater joy, and the holiness of God's presence.

CHAPTER 11

# WE'RE ALL IN THIS TOGETHER

## Caring for Others

Throughout this book, the focus has been on you—what *you* gain and what *you* avoid by cherishing touch. As important as you are, one of the Bible's central messages is that love cannot stop at our own doorstep. "Love your fellow as yourself," God commands us,[1] and not only our "fellow," but the stranger as well.[2] Jewish tradition points out that the Bible begins and ends with acts of kindness—God's provision of clothing for Adam and Eve in Genesis 3:21 and His burial of Moses in Deuteronomy 34:6, to teach us that love of others, expressed not only through feelings but through deeds, should suffuse our lives. This is one reason Judaism eschews asceticism, for one who withdraws from life cannot care for others.[3] Love, Judaism teaches, is a basic principle upon which the entire world stands, and other religions espouse this ethic as well.

Rabbi Jonathan Sacks, former Chief Rabbi of the United Hebrew Congregation of the Commonwealth, comments:

> When the New Testament speaks of love it does so by direct quotation from Leviticus

("You shall love your neighbour as yourself") and Deuteronomy ("You shall love the Lord your God with all your heart, all your soul and all your might"). As philosopher Simon May puts it in his splendid book, *Love: A History*: "The widespread belief that the Hebrew Bible is all about vengeance and 'an eye for an eye,' while the Gospels supposedly invent love as an unconditional and universal value, must therefore count as one of the most extraordinary misunderstandings in all of Western history. For the Hebrew Bible is the source not just of the two love commandments but of a larger moral vision inspired by wonder for love's power." His judgment is unequivocal: "If love in the Western world has a founding text, that text is Hebrew."[4]

Unfortunately, not everyone enters a relationship with other-awareness at the forefront of his or her consciousness. Not everyone stops to think if the pleasurable involvement he or she is anticipating is likely to benefit or, instead, possibly injure the other person. Yet every relationship *does* involve two people, and each person's approach affects the other. If we are to love others, then whether or not we feel we owe it to ourselves to refrain from touch, maybe we owe it to someone else.

There are different issues here for the two sexes. I'll address the females first:

## Respect: A Double-Edged Sword

Ladies, testosterone has undoubtedly given guys a pretty bad rap. "Boys are animals," a high school teacher tells her female students. "Boys are liars," another warns his. Indeed, men have up to 100 times more testosterone circulating in their bodies than women do, and this hormone switches on a part of the brain twice as large as the corresponding part of a woman's brain.[5] No wonder males are more intent on getting physical than women are, particularly during adolescence (and some men have quite an extended adolescence).

Ancient Jewish wisdom describes this gender difference rather succinctly: "Go and learn from the prostitutes' market. Who's hiring whom?" It then continues: "His drive comes from the outside; her drive comes from the inside."[6] Men are more likely to externalize their sexuality, disconnecting it from their internal self, than are women. Furthermore, some indeed will lie ("I really love you," "You can count on me") or at least fudge the truth to get what they want.[7] At the same time, male-bashing is grossly unfair to men, for it reflects only half the story.

The other half (besides the fact that testosterone also fuels a lot of positive energy) is that males, just like females, are *souls*—souls easily distracted by physicality, but souls nonetheless, created in God's image with the desire to do His will. Deep down, these male souls want and need the same thing women do: a committed, loving, lifelong relationship with a soul mate.

So, men have two sides. This is the question that matters:

Which side is activated? Here, women—though they may deny it—have more than a little influence. Ken, a sensitive young man, described it like this:

"We men have an outer will and an inner will. My outer will is for immediate physical pleasure. When a woman is happy to hook up, I'm drawn after my physical instincts, and we both lose: I don't become who I could be, she doesn't get a guy who's interested in her for who she is, and neither of us winds up with a truly satisfying relationship.

"But I also have an inner will. When a woman's behavior compels me to relate to her more deeply, she puts me in touch with the part of me that wants and needs the real thing as much as she does. And we both win."

Ken concluded, "Women have more power than they know."

Politically correct or not, while men are responsible for themselves, women can help bring out the worst or the best in them. Too often, we females act in a way that encourages men to behave like animals—and then we condemn them. If we acted differently, we could help them get in touch with their own higher selves—and we would be the biggest beneficiaries.

Women, be aware of the impact your behavior can have on men, and use it for the good. When you reserve touch for marriage, you just may be serving as a catalyst for another person's spiritual growth. Few things are as gratifying as knowing you helped someone become a more Godlike human being.

## Hey, Sister!

Now for the males:

You probably understand how different men are from most women. Females, on the other hand, have a hard time internalizing this fact. Intellectually, we get it (the whole testosterone thing), but emotionally, we struggle with it. We're wired for closeness—it's been called the "intimacy imperative"[8]—and we want to believe that men relate to us exactly as we relate to them. We often delude ourselves about a man's true intentions. We think he's looking for love when he's looking just to get physical. Furthermore, "getting physical" often means more than what a girl has in mind at the moment. Have you ever heard the Beatles' song "I Wanna Hold Your Hand"? It was a hit precisely because women fell for it. No male has ever seen a beautiful woman and said to himself, "Wow—I'd sure like to hold her hand!"

Women, like men, have hormones. Nevertheless, a healthy, non-desensitized woman can't relate to a man only externally. For females, physical and emotional go together.

A speaker I know once made this point in the following way:

"Guys," she addressed the male half of the audience, "imagine this: You're in a restaurant when an incredibly beautiful woman comes in and sits down at the table next to yours. She opens her mouth—and says something really stupid. She opens her mouth again—and again she says something really stupid. And a third time. And a fourth, and a fifth. You may not want to marry her—but I bet she's still looking just as good."

Grins.

"Now, ladies," she continued, "you're in a restaurant when an absolutely gorgeous guy comes in and sits down at the table next to yours. He opens his mouth—and he says something really stupid. You don't have to wait to hear more. Suddenly, his attractiveness has plummeted, and any relationship you may have fantasized about having with him has gone up in smoke. Am I right?"

Vigorous nods.

If every man with little to offer besides his looks would obligingly say something stupid right away, as in the above example, women would be a lot better off. Unfortunately, this doesn't always happen. Here we arrive at the key point. Because women do have hormones but can't act on them without at least some accompanying feelings, they rely on their fertile and eager imaginations to create a reason for those feelings. Consequently, as long as an attractive guy doesn't immediately say or do something to disqualify himself, a woman will invest him with all sorts of imaginary virtues so she can feel better about where her hormones are taking her. (Once she's gotten there, any stupid remarks he makes will probably sound cute.)

The upshot is that women are more prone to this type of self-delusion then men, and inevitably suffer the consequences. A woman is more likely to want to see something, believe she sees it, and, based on this illusion, devote herself physically and emotionally to someone ridiculously inappropriate for her. After however long, when he says, "Thanks, it's been fun, and I hope you didn't take things too seriously," she can be badly hurt.

So guys, do women an important kindness. Don't take advantage of their vulnerabilities. Don't tempt a woman into a relationship she doesn't need. Ask yourself if you would be happy if someone treated your mother, your sister or your future wife the way you are about to treat this woman. If the answer is no, your behavior is about to damage one of God's creations.

Do *yourself* an important kindness as well. Remember that your outer will—your drive for immediate physical pleasure—pulls you away from your deepest needs and desires, while your inner will directs you to fulfill them. When you're in the company of a female, ask yourself, "*Which will is she activating?*" It it's your outer will, *leave*. You don't need this relationship any more than she does. Just as you shouldn't want to damage her, you shouldn't want to damage yourself.

> *Cherishing touch is one of the kindest things anyone can do for anybody.*

In the final analysis, both males and females are created in the image of God and both deserve to be treated with respect and compassion. Both men and women suffer from relationships gone wrong. Cherishing touch is one of the kindest things anyone can do for anybody.

An old friend of mine named Jodi had an experience that drove this point home to her. Traveling through Europe, she met a young Italian named Antonio. The two liked each other immediately, got physically involved and spent a few romantic days together. Jodi's affection for Antonio, however, wasn't enough to keep her in Italy while her Eurail Pass expired. She bade him goodbye, confident that their relationship would leave him with no more than fond memories.

She was wrong. Three months later, back at home, she found a letter from Italy in her mailbox.

"I feel so sad and lonely ever since you left," Antonio wrote. "I think of you every waking moment, and each day I'm falling more and more in love with you."

At first, Jodi was flattered. That feeling soon gave way to dismay as she realized, "Oh, no—what have I done?"

To Jodi, their brief relationship had seemed harmless. Antonio had known she wouldn't be staying. Nonetheless, she had unwittingly encouraged a full-fledged infatuation, and now she felt largely responsible for his unhappiness.

Antonio's story, fortunately, was fairly tame. He didn't respond to the loss of the relationship as others have done, by becoming clinically depressed, cutting himself, or developing an eating disorder. Nor did he leave Italy to follow his "love," giving up his studies or his job, abandoning his own life path for her—which, had Jodi loved him, she wouldn't have permitted.

Indeed, in time, Antonio was able to get over Jodi and move

on, eventually marrying. But as Jodi became more sensitive to physical relationships, she realized that he could regain his happiness but never that measure of singularity and specialness he would otherwise have known with his wife—and his wife would likewise never have a husband who would have memories only of her. While Jodi knew she was not Antonio's only such romance, she deeply regretted her part in his loss.

Few of us may feel as strongly as Jodi did. Perhaps we should. A person who knows how bad smoking is may lack the willpower to quit, but he or she still may not want to give someone else a cigarette. Similarly, however much or little concern you feel for yourself, you're probably sensitive enough to feel for others. Rather than damaging them, you want to help them get the best out of life, which means, among other things, helping them actualize everything we've discussed. You want to help them develop an appreciation of reality that will increase their chances of entering into a relationship with the right person, someone they can love for a lifetime. You want to spare them pain, disillusionment and desensitization. You want to enable them to enjoy as much specialness as possible with their God-given soul mate.

When you reserve physical closeness for your ultimate relationship, you are doing much more than simply looking out for your own interests. Cherishing touch shows that you care not only about yourself but also about others.

## What Does This Mean for Dating?

*How can you realistically have a long-term relationship without touching? If you can't, then what are you supposed to do?*

When I speak to young adults for whom dating (or "variations" on dating, such as hooking up) is the norm—which is about 99% of young adults—I try to discuss only the issue of refraining from touch, skirting the larger issue of male-female relationships. However, when it inevitably comes up, I don't mince words.

At the end of one of my talks, a religious eighteen-year-old girl named Sarah asked pointedly, "So when do you think I should start dating?"

"Do you intend to save touch for marriage?" I asked her just as pointedly.

"Yes."

"When do you think you'll be ready for marriage?"

"Well, I want to finish college first, so probably when I'm around twenty-two."

"How long do you think you could go out with a guy you're feeling closer and closer to and still not touch, including engagement?"

Sarah thought a moment. "Maybe, if I'm really strong, six months."

"So start dating when you're twenty-one and a half."

At least this girl thought about timing a relationship before becoming involved in it. Other people don't. Once after I spoke on a program for college students, a young woman introduced herself as Dana.

"My boyfriend and I have decided to try reserving touch for marriage," she told me. "We're hoping you can help us get started."

"I'd be happy to, if I can," I replied. "Tell me a little about your relationship."

"Well, we're very close," Dana began. "We're both sophomores at the same university and have the same major, so we attend many of the same classes. We often study together. In fact, we probably spend most of our waking hours together. We plan to get married in two and half years, after graduation. We really love each other."

She paused. "So what practical advice can you give us about how <u>not</u> to touch?"

I shook my head sympathetically. "Beats me."

Refraining from touch with the person whom you intend to marry is intended for a relatively brief period prior to the wedding. That means delaying dating until you're ready to get married, and once you've found the right person, setting a date for as soon as possible. Otherwise you're asking for trouble.

I once got a letter from a very distressed young girl. "I became friendly with my boyfriend when I was twelve," Suzanne wrote. "We were just friends for nearly two years. But a while ago we realized we have stronger feelings for each other. This is not some teenage infatuation—we're more mature than most people our age. We genuinely know and love each other. We're certain we're right for each other.

"The problem is, we're only fourteen—and I can't imagine getting married until I'm at least twenty. We haven't touched and I don't want to start. But how are we supposed to survive like this for the next six years?"

What could I possibly tell Suzanne? Break up, and pick up things in five and a half years? Don't break up, but hardly see each other, and meet only in broad daylight and in crowded places? Any practical answer would be emotionally unacceptable.

Yet staying in a long-term relationship and hoping to continue not touching is equally impractical. Even dating for a shorter period but spending too much time together can send the best of intentions down the drain. This happened to a nearly engaged couple I know—and although they recommitted to not touching until they were married, they had to deal with mutual blame, mistrust and loss of respect in the wake of what had happened. Setbacks like this can derail a relationship.

Then there are negative consequences of a different sort. I know of a young couple who were committed to not touching, and who were seeing far too much of each other during their very long engagement. The tension grew unbearable, so they adopted a desperate coping mechanism: They shut off the romantic energy between them and began relating as brother and sister. After marrying, they had major problems getting the romance back.

The above assumes that couples who embark upon a relationship when very young are still an appropriate match when they're ready to marry. While it's sweet to hear of couples who met in middle school and are now celebrating their fiftieth anniversary, far more common are couples who were well suited as teenagers but whose lives later take different directions. Eventually and painfully, they realize that a connection they thought would last a lifetime, didn't—and physical involvement exacerbates the situation.

A distraught young woman once called me with this problem: She's twenty, she said, and has had a boyfriend for three years. Now she's starting to think about marriage—and it's clear that this guy is not The One. At the same time, she's been physical with him, loves him, and can't imagine leaving him. She's torn. What should she do?

Obviously, she can't marry the wrong person because of an emotional attachment. There's no choice but to say a painful goodbye to Mr. Wrong and hope to find Mr. Right. What a shame it is that she invested so much in a relationship that couldn't endure—and how agonizing to break up.

"But he *could* have been the right guy," you may protest. True. And you can jump into a physical relationship with someone you barely know, and he or she *could* be your soul mate. For that matter, you can cross a busy street blindfolded and *could* make it safely to the other side. Intelligent people don't live that way.

The kinds of problems I've described are why relationships are an extremely risky business. Please don't think, in all innocence, "Well, then how about just texting a guy/girl or chatting on Facebook?" "Talking" via texting or Facebook can lead to talking on the phone, which can lead to talking in person in well-lit public places, which can lead to talking in *not* well-lit, *not* public places, which can lead to *not* talking... As ancient Jewish wisdom states: "No one can guarantee another's sexual innocence."[9] Put more colloquially, "Don't trust yourself." As a friend of mine says, "Every office affair begins with a casual conversation at the water cooler."

In addition, believe it or not, just gazing into someone's eyes and connecting emotionally can cause a feel-good oxytocin response.[10] In other words, females (and higher-oxytocin males) bond just by talking. (Ever wonder why teenage girls spend so much time on the phone?) Plus the guy may interpret it as more than talking: One study found that when a man observes a man and woman conversing, the sexual areas of his brain are activated.[11] What women see as an innocent conversation, men perceive as a potential physical encounter.

> *What women see as an innocent conversation, men perceive as a potential physical encounter.*

The upshot: There's nothing simple about male-female interaction—and, as I've tried to show, about where it leads. Conclusion: There's no point in involving yourself in relationships until you're ready for the real thing.

I once addressed a group of eighteen-year-old boys from somewhat religious homes on this topic, and as the discussion progressed, they grew less and less happy. By the time I concluded, I beheld a silent room of extremely glum faces. Finally, someone in the front row raised his hand.

"If I've understood correctly," he said slowly, "you've said dating should be for marriage. None of us here is ready to get married. So"—he paused, almost afraid to continue—"does that mean... are you saying... none of us should be dating?"

No point in beating around the bush. "You got it," I replied.

There was a moment's silence as the terrible truth sank in. Then, looking totally forlorn, he asked, "Well, what are we supposed to be doing?"

I'll tell you what you're supposed to be doing: Use these years as a time to work on yourself. Take all the energy you would otherwise spend checking out the cutest guy or girl at the pizza shop, and use it to become as good, giving and growing a human being as possible. Develop your social networks, especially meaningful friendships. Be altruistic. (As a fringe benefit, both socializing and altruism will give you an oxytocin boost, especially when done together, as in group volunteer work.) Increase your spiritual activities. All of these activities will make you a richer and deeper person. In short, become worthy of marrying someone amazing. Then date to find the person with whom to share all you have become—for a lifetime.

Especially if you want to cherish touch, it makes the most sense to reserve dating for the loftiest purpose there is: finding your soul mate.

CONCLUSION

# CONCLUSION: MOVING FORWARD

I live on the western edge of Jerusalem, and often go out on my balcony to gaze at the beautiful mountains surrounding this amazing city. The hills are ancient, but the trees that forest them are new—hand-planted over the past century by pioneers determined to reclaim a barren land. They are a sign of rebirth and hope, of the belief that this Land has a promising and beautiful future.

Just as those early pioneers were pulled back to the Land by a renewed Jewish nationalism, today more and more people are being pulled back to the wisdom rooted in Judaism's 3,000-year-old counterculture by the desire for meaningful lives and meaningful relationships. In traditional religious values, whether spoken in the name of Judaism or their own faiths, they are finding a refreshingly liberating sexual morality that is giving them hope for their own futures.

Indeed, after the cultural upheaval caused by the sexual revolution, social scientists are finally "discovering" what most religions have known all along. "Relationships that start slowly are more satisfying in the end," researchers recently reported, based on a study of over 600 couples. Traditional courtship, it turns out, gives people time to get to really know each other and assess their compatibility without their judgment being clouded. Acting on strong sexual desire, we're told, "may thwart the development of other key ingredients of a healthy relationship such as commitment, mutual understanding, or shared values." The conclusion? Couples who take their time are happier—and have better sex lives—than those who jump in physically.[1]

Yet many of us continue "to put the cart before the horse." The result is a depressing resignation pervading the relationships scene. If you're like most people I've met, you realize things aren't working—yet you wonder sadly if anything can be done. Maybe you feel stuck, bound by social expectations, by "the way things are." Maybe you're also afraid of being socially isolated.

"It all made so much sense when you spoke," a woman wrote me. "But back here on campus, it's another world. I know the system's not working, and most people aren't happy. But 'cherishing touch' simply isn't feasible here."

I had just finished reading an interesting and very disturbing book about traditional Chinese women.

"Imagine this," I wrote back. "You are traveling through China and come across a small village where life is essentially the same as it was a century ago. There you meet an illiterate 15-year-old girl. In a year, she'll be forced to marry a man whom her parents selected long ago and in whom she has no interest. She'll be expected to serve him like a slave.

## Conclusion: Moving Forward

That, basically, will be her life.

"She listens wide-eyed as you describe your world. You tell her that women in your society are fully educated and can pursue any field. They choose when and whom they'll marry, and aspire to a relationship based upon mutual respect and love.

" 'It all makes so much sense,' she says with a sigh. 'But where I live, it's another world. I know the system is unjust, and I'm unlikely to end up happy. But getting an education and having the kind of marriage you describe just isn't feasible here.'

"I think you'd reply, 'Listen to me! We're talking about your life! If you can't get what you want here, then get out!' "

Tragically, such a young woman may find it practically impossible to pick up and leave. Unlike her, however, most of us have considerable freedom. The question is whether we exercise it. When "the system isn't working," we can "go with the flow"—or move, at our own pace, toward a more intelligent and rewarding way of living. We can play by the "rules" of the surrounding culture—or dare to be different, with all the benefits of that difficult choice. It's up to us. If you do have courage, you may find that you are less alone than you think.

> *When "the system isn't working," we can "go with the flow"—or move, at our own pace, toward a more intelligent and rewarding way of living.*

## Counter-Cultural Stirrings

Every year, around Valentine's Day, students at my alma mater run a university-sponsored, campus-wide event called Sex Week at Yale. Featuring such experts as sex toy manufacturers and porn stars, it is a weeklong celebration of utterly raw and crude physicality. (I wanted to learn more about it, but my internet filter wouldn't let me.)

In protest, some students formed a group called Undergraduates for a Better Yale College. Here's what they have to say on their website:

> *We believe Yale can do better. We exist, therefore, to advocate for a better sexual culture, one grounded in genuine respect and self-giving love; to oppose campus attitudes and events that offer a degrading and trivializing vision of sexuality; and to embody the alternative in our personal lives to the best of our abilities. We stand for a Yale where sexual objectification is unknown, where freshmen are not pressured to accept inebriated hook-ups as the default lifestyle, and where students' romantic lives teach them to love and respect the whole person, not just the body or particular parts thereof.*[2]

This group accordingly sponsored a competing event called True Love Week, with guest speakers on topics such as "Sexual Bliss: Satisfaction and *Marital* [italics added] Happiness for Today's Couples" and "The Person as a Gift." They also sponsored the Great Date Night, in which you actually "ask somebody out to a fun evening and get to know them the old-fashioned way" in order to "begin to build a base of shared experiences" (and they don't mean sexual). In their literature, they say:

> *Nervous? Well, maybe, but if sex and heavy drinking are left aside for the night, there is at least no reason to be distracted or have ulterior motives. You can simply focus on getting to know the other person.*[3]

Getting to know the other person? Boy, that sounds radical. But is it really? "That which has been is that which shall be, and that which has been done is that which shall be done," King Solomon wrote 2,000 years ago. "There is nothing new under the sun."[4] If those who believe in "cherishing touch" are considered radical, it's only because we have finally come full circle, where our thinking has become so progressive that it has ended up meeting ancient wisdom.

*If you want to adopt a more wholesome sexual ethic than that which prevails today, don't make the mistake of thinking you're alone.*

At the same time, "cherishing touch" is definitely counter-cultural in today's world. Counter-cultural used to mean trashing tradition, putting love on the back burner and going for sex. Today it means embracing tradition, putting sex on the back burner and going for love.

If you want to adopt a more wholesome sexual ethic than that which prevails today, don't make the mistake of thinking you're alone. Studies have revealed that the hookup scene is fueled in part by "pluralistic ignorance": both men and women hook up because they overestimate others' comfort with it, not realizing how many people have the same qualms they do.[5]

The fact is that all of us, having been created in God's image, have far more latent spirituality than we appreciate. Could it actually be that, in fearing being "the only one," we may be underestimating others? Plenty of sensitive souls out there may very well be open to trying something different—if only someone would show them the way.

Imagine yourself out with a very attractive person. It's getting late, the energy between you is good, and it feels natural to take that exciting step into a physical relationship. But you stop a minute. You take a deep breath. And then you look into his or her eyes and say: "You know, you're the most beautiful woman/man I've ever met, and part of me would love to get physically involved with you right now. But there's something I believe in—it's called 'not selling either of us short.' So how about if we wait, get to know each other better, and see what there really could be between us."

If a man had said that to me when I was single, once I got over my shock, I would have been overwhelmed with awe and admiration. In fact, I probably would have fallen at his feet. A man's response to such a speech might be less enthusiastic, but if he really likes you—and if he's worth anything—he'll rise to the challenge. If not, what have you lost? Move on and find someone who's interested in you for who you are.

Whether you're male or female, you just might spark a real spiritual awakening in the other person—and given the genuine relationship that may then develop, who knows how great your reward will be?

# ACKNOWLEDGMENTS

Several people were crucial in helping this book see the light of day. Although I'd dreamed of getting it out into the world for years, Cynthia Kersey's inspiring book *Unstoppable* got me off my tush (that's Jewish for bottom) and gave me the determination to turn the dream into reality. My ever-loving, supportive, and (unlike me) practical husband Avraham suggested I e-mail everyone I know to ask for suggestions and contacts. Frances Gozland responded and put me in touch with Ari Lapin, who put me in touch with his father. After getting to know Rabbi Daniel Lapin through an enlivening and enlightening e-mail exchange, I was convinced he was the person of integrity and vision I wanted to publish my book. (While he remembers having persuaded me, I don't recall needing much persuasion.) Rabbi Lapin's wife Susan then entered the picture, and her impressive perceptivity, sensitivity, and editorial skills raised my concept of professionalism to new heights. Getting to know and working with the Lapins has been a pleasure and a rare privilege. Finally, John Lewis and Christian Ophus crowned the project with their outstanding cover design which, when I saw it, plastered a huge smile on my face for the whole day.

I thank all these all people from the bottom of my heart.

Above all, I thank Hashem (God) for showering so many undeserved blessings upon me. My life of Torah, my wonderful husband, seven precious children, deeply rewarding work, amazing friends and teachers, a home in Jerusalem—and now the birth of this book. It's more than anything I could ever have hoped for, and I am eternally grateful.

# END NOTES

CHAPTER 1

1. Laura Sessions Stepp, *Unhooked: How Young Women Pursue Sex, Delay Love, and Lose at Both* (NY: Riverhood Books, 2007), p. 122.

2. Isaiah 42:6, 49:6, 60:3.

3. Genesis 2:18.

CHAPTER 2

1. See A. Schirmer, K. Teh, S. Wang, R. Vijoyakumar, A. Ching, D. Nithanthem, N. Escoffier, and A. Cheok, "Squeeze Me, But Don't Tease Me: Human and Mechanical Touch Enhance Visual Attention and Emotional Discrimination." *Social Neuroscience* (2011) 6 (3), 219–230.

2. Babylonian Talmud, tractates Ketubot 8a, Eruvin 18a.

3. Zohar (Book of Splendor), chapter Mishpatim.

4. Louann Brizendine, M.D., *The Female Brain* (NY: Morgan Road Books, 2006), pp. 101-02.

5. Ibid., p. 106, citing Kerstin Uvnäs-Moberg, "Oxytocin May Mediate the Benefits of Positive Social Interaction and Emotion," *Psychoneuroendocrinology* 23 (November 1988) (8):819-35; and citing Kerstin Uvnäs-Moberg, *The Oxytocin Factor* (NY: Perseus, 2003).

6. Ibid., p. 82.

7. Ibid., pp. 67-68, 71-72.

8. Mauricio Delgado, "To Trust or Not to Trust: Ask Oxytocin," *Scientific American*, July 15, 2008.

9. J.A. Barazza, M. E. McCullough, S. Ahmadi, and P. J. Zak, "Oxytocin Infusion Increases Charitable Donations Regardless of Monetary Resources," *Hormones and Behavior* 60 (2011) 148-51.

10. Brizendine, *Female Brain*, p. 68, citing K. C. Light et al., "More Frequent Partner Hugs and Higher Oxytocin Levels Are Linked to Lower Blood Pressure and Vascular Resistance during Stress in Post-Menopausal Women on Estrogen Replacement," *Hormonal Behavior* 47 (2005) (5): 540-48; and citing C. S. Carter, "Neuroendocrine Perspectives on Social Attachment and Love," *Psychoneuroendocrinology* 23 (1998) (8): 779-818; Susan Kuchinskas, *The Chemistry of Connection: How the Oxytocin Response Can Help You Find Trust, Intimacy, and Love* (Oakland: New Harbinger Publications, 2009), p. 86.

11. Brizendine, *Female Brain*, p. 68.
12. Kuchinskas, *Chemistry of Connection*, p. 18.
13. Ibid., p. 119.
14. Ibid., pp. 121–22.
15. Brizendine, *Female Brain*, p. 39.
16. This attachment is fueled by the hormone vasopressin, which is triggered by vigilance and aggression. (See Kuchinskas, pp. 17, 121-22.)
17. Kuchinskas, *Chemistry of Connection*, p. 103, citing P. B. Gray et al., "Social Variables Predict Between-Subject but Not Day-to-Day Variation in the Testosterone of U.S. Men," *Psychoneuroendocrinology* 29 (2004) (9): 1153–62.
18. Wendy Shalit, *Girls Gone Mild: Young Women Reclaim Self-Respect and Find It's Not Bad to Be Good* (NY: Random House, 2007), p. 201, citing Ron Louis and David Copeland, *How to Succeed with Women* (NY: Reward, 1998), p. 206. [*Girls Gone Mild* was later republished as *The Good Girl Revolution: Young Rebels with Self-Esteem and High Standards* (NY: Ballantine, 2008).]
19. See Michael Gurian, *The Wonder of Girls: Understanding the Hidden Nature of Our Daughters* (NY: Atria Books, 2002), p. 269.
20. Miriam Grossman, M.D., *Unprotected: A Campus Psychiatrist Reveals How Political Correctness in Her Profession Endangers Every Student* (NY: Sentinel, 2007), p. 4, citing A. Levine and J. Cureton, "What We Know about Today's College Students," *About Campus*, March–April 1998.
21. Herman Wouk, *This Is My God* (Garden City, NY: Doubleday & Company, Inc., 1959), p. 155.

CHAPTER 4

1. Judith S. Wallerstein and Sandra Blakeslee, *The Good Marriage: How and Why Love Lasts* (NY: Warner Books, 1995), p. 47.
2. Louann Brizendine, *The Female Brain* (NY: Morgan Road Books, 2006), p. 66, citing A. Aron et al., "Reward, Motivation, and Emotion Systems Associated with Early-Stage Intense Romantic Love," *Journal of Neurophysiology* 94 (2005) (1): 327–37.
3. Brizendine, *Female Brain*, p. 66, citing T. R. Insel and R. D. Fernald, "How the Brain Processes Social Information: Searching for the Social Brain," *Annual Review of Neuroscience* 27 (2004): 697–722.
4. Susan Kuchinskas, *The Chemistry of Connection: How the Oxytocin Response Can Help You Find Trust, Intimacy, and Love*

# End Notes

(Oakland: New Harbinger Publications, 2009), p. 78.

5. See Kuchinskas, *Chemistry of Connection*, pp. 19, 55, and ch. 7; and Susan Kuchinskas, "Recovering from MDMA Burnout," May 24, 2009 post on http://hugthemonkey.com.

## CHAPTER 5

1. Quoted in *She Said, She Said: Strong Words from Strong-Minded Women* (NY: Avon Books, 1995), p. 34.

## CHAPTER 6

1. See, for example, S. L. Murray, J. G. Holmes, and D. W. Griffin, "The Self-Fulfilling Nature of Positive Illusions in Romantic Relationships: Love Is Not Blind, but Prescient." http://web.psych.utoronto.ca/gmacdonald/WebFollowUp/Murray Holmes%Griffin.pdf.

2. See Erich Fromm, *The Art of Loving* (NY: Perennial Library, 1956).

3. Rabbi Eliyahu Eliezer Dessler, *Michtav Me'Eliyahu*, vol. 1, "*Kuntras HaChessed*" [Booklet on Lovingkindness] (B'nei Brak: Committee for the Publication of the Writings of Rabbi E. E. Dessler, 1984). [English: *Strive for Truth* (Jerusalem: Feldheim Publishers, 1978).]

4. Psalms 89:3.

5. Dr. Jill Murray, *But I Love Him: Protecting Your Daughter from Controlling, Abusive Dating Relationships* (NY: HarperCollins, 2000).

## CHAPTER 7

1. *Bereshit Rabbah* 18:1, based on Genesis 22:2.

## CHAPTER 8

1. From *Naked Truths and Veiled Illusions*, quoted in *She Said, She Said: Strong Words from Strong-Minded Women* (NY: Avon Books, 1995), p. 34.

2. *Wikipedia*, "Relationships," citing David M. Buss, *Evolutionary Psychology* (NY: Atlyn & Bacon, 1999), p. 154.

3. Wendy Shalit, *A Return to Modesty: Reclaiming the Lost Virtue* (NY: The Free Press, 1999), p. 53, citing James B. Allen et al., "Influence of Popular Erotica on Judgments of Strangers and Mates," *Journal of Experimental Social Psychology* 25 (1989) (2): 159–67.

4. Babylonian Talmud, tractate Pesachim 112b–113a.

5. Michael Gurian, *The Wonder of Girls: Understanding the Hidden Nature of Our Daughters* (NY: Atria Books, 2002), pp. 36, 61.

6. Babylonian Talmud, Berachot 34b.

CHAPTER 9

1. Babylonian Talmud, tractate Niddah 30b.

CHAPTER 10

1. Wendy Shalit, *A Return to Modesty: Discovering the Lost Virtue* (NY: Free Press, 1999), pp. 163-167.

2. Susan Kuchinskas, *The Chemistry of Connection: How the Oxytocin Response Can Help You Find Trust, Intimacy, and Love* (Oakland: New Harbinger Publications, 2009), pp. 21-22.

3. Susan Kuchinskas, "The Oxytocin Gap," August 14. 2009 post on http://hugthe monkey.com.

4. Kuchinskas, *Chemistry of Connection*, pp. 3, 45.

5. Wendy Shalit, *Girls Gone Mild: Young Women Reclaim Self-Respect and Find It's Not Bad to Be Good* (NY: Random House, 2007), p. 100. [Later republished as *The Good Girl Revolution: Young Rebels with Self-Esteem and High Standards* (NY: Ballantine, 2008).]

6. "Dr. Rebecca Turner Issues Statement Rebutting 'Pseudoscience'," http://www.newswise.com/articles/dr-rebecca-turner-issues-statement-rebutting-pseudoscience. Released 11/20/2006.

7. Kuchinskas, "Oxytocin Gap."

8. Susan Kuchinskas, "More on Dr. Keroack's Theories of Oxytocin," December 4, 2006 post on hugthemonkey.com, citing research of Dr. Rebecca Turner.

9. Kuchinckas, "Oxytocin Gap" and comments.

10. Genesis 24:67.

CHAPTER 11

1. Leviticus 19:18.

2. Leviticus 19:33-34.

3. Michael Kaufman, *Love, Marriage, and Family in Jewish Law and Tradition* (NY: Jason Aaronson, 1992), p. 85.

4. Rabbi Jonathan Sacks, weekly e-mail "Covenant and Conversation," August 11, 2012, citing Simon May, *Love: A History* (Yale University Press, 2011), 14, 19-20.

5. Louann Brizendine, *The Female Brain* (NY: Morgan Road Books, 2006), pp. 89, 91.

6. Babylonian Talmud, tractate Ketubot 64b.

7. Brizendine, *Female Brain*, p. 64, citing David Buss, "Psychological

Sex Differences: Origins through Sexual Selection," *American Psychology American Psychology* 50 (1995) (3): 164-68, discussion 169-71; and citing W. Tooke, "Patterns of Deception in Intersexual Mating Strategies," *Ethology and Sociobiology* 12 (1991) (5): 345-64.

8. Michael Gurian, *The Wonder of Girls: Understanding the Hidden Nature of Our Daughters* (NY: Atria Books, 2002), pp. 23, 53-55.

9. Babylonian Talmud, Ketubot 13b.

10. Brizendine, *Female Brain* (NY: Morgan Road Books, 2006), p. 68, citing Kerstin Uvnäs-Moberg, *The Oxytocin Factor* (NY: Persues, 2003); and citing Rebecca Anne Turner et al., "Preliminary Research on Plasma Oxytocin in Normal Cycling Women: Investigating Emotion and Interpersonal Distress," *Psychiatry* 62 (1999) (2) 97-113; Susan Kunchinskas, *The Chemistry of Connection: How the Oxytocin Response Can Help You Find Trust, Intimacy, and Love* (Oakland: New Harbinger Publications, 2009), p. 143, citing Paul J. Zak, "Trust: A Temporary Human Attachment Facilitated by Oxtyocin," *Behavioral and Brain Sciences* 28 (2005) (3): 368-69.

11. Brizendine, *Female Brain*, p. 5, citing Steven W. Gangestad and Randy Thornhill, "Menstrual Cycle Variation in Women's Preferences for the Scent of Symmetrical Men," *Proceedings, Biological Sciences* 265 (1988) (1339): 927-33; and citing Deborah Tannen, "Gender Differences in Topical Coherence: Creating Involvement in Best Friends' Talk," *Discourse Processes: Special Gender and Conversational Interaction* 13 (1990) (1):73-90. See also Guéguen, "The Effect of a Woman's Incidental Tactile Contact on Men's Later Behavior," 263, citing A. Abbey, "Misperceptions of Friendly Behavior as Sexual Interest: A Survey of Naturally Occurring Incidents," *Psychology of Women Quarterly* 11 (1987): 173-94.

CONCLUSION

1. Fiona Macrae, "You Can't Hurry Love: Abstain in the Bedroom in the Early Days of a Relationship If You Want It to Last," *Daily Mail* (UK), September 2, 2012.

2. http://betteryale.org.

3. Ibid.

4. Ecclesiastes 1:9.

5. C. Reiber and J. R. Garcia, "Hooking Up: Gender Differences, Evolution, and Pluralistic Ignorance," *Evolutionary Psychology*, July 24, 2010, 8(3): 390-404. See also T. A. Lambert, A. S. Kahn, and K. J. Apple, "Pluralistic Ignorance and Hooking Up," *Journal of Sex Research*, May 2003, 40(2):129-33.

| LIFECODEX PUBLISHING PRESENTS |

# Would you like access to more insights from ancient Jewish wisdom?

 **Sign up to receive a FREE *Thought Tool* every week!**

*Thought Tools* is a free weekly email from Rabbi Daniel Lapin. This short message brings you spiritual tips, techniques, and knowledge that you can use to improve your life in four areas: family, faith, friends, and finances.

Regardless of your background, *Thought Tools* offers you fascinating glimpses into the Lord's language – Hebrew, little-known secrets from Ancient Jewish Wisdom, information on Jewish holidays and customs, Bible secrets, and other mystical traditions with practical implications.

Expand your range of consciousness and spark conversation with family and friends by sharing these nuggets of wisdom.

Sign up for *Thought Tools* at
**www.rabbidaniellapin.com**

*"The more things change, the more we depend on those things that never change. That's why you need a rabbi."*

— Rabbi Daniel Lapin

# ENJOY THESE ADDITIONAL BOOKS AND AUDIO CDS FROM LIFECODEX PUBLISHING

www.RabbiDanielLapin.com

Video DVD

## Ancient Jewish Wisdom – Vol. 2

For many years, Rabbi Daniel and Susan Lapin have been on a mission to make ancient Jewish wisdom accessible to all. After receiving so many emails and letters about their TV show on the TCT television network, Rabbi Daniel and Susan Lapin are delighted to make four of their favorite shows available to you on this DVD.

Going beneath the surface of Scripture, they bring Biblical verses to life as they explore the original Hebrew wording and share lessons from over 3,000 years of oral transmission. Join the thousands who have benefited by watching these shows and applying the practical, real-life messages to their own lives.

Hardcover Book

## Thou Shall Prosper (2nd Edition): Ten Commandments for Making Money

*Thou Shall Prosper* explains:
- Why Jews throughout the ages flourish economically
- How you can benefit from this Jewish wisdom
- What "being in business" means, whether you are a professional, a CEO or flipping burgers
- Why you should never retire

One Audio CD

## Perils of Profanity

### You Are What You Speak

- How vulgar speech damages your chances for success in both business and personal relationships
- Why Joseph recounted his dreams to his brothers, knowing that they would be angered
- What damage to the soul comes from using or hearing profanity
- Why everyone, even those who don't curse, should be concerned about the prevalence of foul language in our culture

# GILA MANOLSON

Gila Manolson was born into an assimilated Jewish family in the northeastern United States. Considering herself an atheist, she expressed her idealism through social causes, including vegetarianism, feminism, and environmentalism. After graduating Yale University and traveling through Europe, she found herself in Jerusalem, where she discovered a "3000-year-old counterculture" — Torah Judaism. Intrigued by its teachings, she decided to stay and study, and never left.

Gila has always been interested in the topic of male-female relationships. Unimpressed by how they were conducted in the secular world, she made it her goal to understand the traditional Jewish approach. The incredible response to her speeches around the world has led her to writing this book in the hope of encouraging more people to enjoy healthy and joyful lives.

Stay in touch with Gila at www.rabbidaniellapin.com